MW00444308

Abstract

Higher order critical thinking is an implied goal for all schools participating in the academic frame of the International Baccalaureate (IB) curriculum. Being a gifted student enrolled in the IB does not, however, guarantee higher order thinking will be achieved. This study articulated, through student voice, the potential effectiveness of transcendental teaching styles in the IB system, and how that style might become the platform to attain higher orders of cognitive ability. Embedded as a problem among the reasons for this ambition not being successfully accomplished is a possible reliance on traditional education approaches that miss the transcendent culture of ephemeral inspiration. Understanding that the IB curriculum is designed to help students' articulate complex ideas in relevant contexts, this inquiry-based study identified unachieved higher sublimations of thought among learners exploration of ideas, questions and perspectives related to higher level critical awareness. Therefore, the purpose of this phenomenological research study was to recognize the distinctions of transcendental learning and why higher order thinking was not being achieved within the IB. This study utilized qualitative research methods that focused on phenomenology as the best way to consider the descriptions of interrelated student environments providing interpretations of influences accordingly. . The research was an inquiry- method phenomenology addressing the need to recognize student voice which may have been marginalized in practice. The end goal framed the researcher's interpretations of the participants in their day-to-day academic life. The IB graduated student participants associated with the study were five graduated IB students who have completed college and are currently in the workplace.

List of Tables

Chapter 1: Introduction

The phenomena of Transcendental Education (TE) and the International Baccalaureate (IB) are comingled as a learning arrangement designed to service higher order thinking skills (Aktas, & Guven, 2015; Budsankom, Sawangboon, Damrongpanit & Chuensirimongkol 2015). The creation of the IB came from the thoughts of Robert Leach who followed the education theories of John Dewey 1895-1952, A.S. Smith 1883-1973, Jean Piaget 1896-1980, and Jerome Bruner 1915 – present (International Baccalaureate, 2016). Robert Leach, as the original promoter of the International Baccalaureate (IB), organized the Conference of Internationally-minded Schools (International Baccalaureate, 2016). Succeeding the inspiration of Robert Leach the International Schools Association (ISA) conference of teachers of international social studies recommended that their International Passport to Higher Education be called "International Baccalaureate." The IB evolved into an international non-profit education foundation organization formally recognized with non-profit status in 1968 (International Baccalaureate, 2016). The impetus of the IB focus was on the belief that cross disciplinary education moved the IB closer to encouraging students across the world to become active lifelong learners (Park, Caine & Wimmer, 2014).

The IB included a global mix by appending a Diploma Program (DP) within IB giving the IB organization a platform for multi-cultural understanding best explained by Robert Rauschenberg as "There are so many interesting ways to be other than right" (Rauschenberg, personal communication, August 18, 1959). To achieve this unsegregated world view of the IB DP, discursive intellectualism within IB became an important skill necessary for success in the post-secondary environment as well as the workplace (Park, Caine & Wimmer, 2014). Students inside the IB demonstrate discursive intellectual values congruent with care, correctness, significance, consequence, and the socialization of applied scholarly culture (Smith & Morgan, 2010).

The impact of the IB is mentioned a great deal in literature (Corlu, 2014; Fitzgerald, 2015; Jamal, 2016; Kadıoğlu, & Erişen, 2016). However, research also shows that IB programs routinely fail to deliver an education outcome beyond the scaled rubric of quantitative prescription (Tarc & Beatty, 2012). This failure can impede students from developing the skill to enjoy the synergism of higher-order thinking (Cole, Ullman, Gannon & Rooney, 2015). While not all students need to experience synergism in their education experience, students who possess exceptional skills should be challenged by the demands of course administrators and teachers (Grant, 2016). Furthermore, these students require teaching faculty to emphasize areas of study leading to cognitive critical thinking (Kwan, & Wong, 2015). By design, the IB programs are integrated in to general classroom environments (Jamal, 2016). The purpose is so the IB is accessible as a cohort within the general classroom. However, the imbedding of the IB program in the general classroom may contribute to a disruption of transcendental education (Cole et. al., 2015).

Background

Effective learning that leads to higher order thinking available to the IB student should be coalesced with critical thinking (Budsankom, Sawangboon, Damrongpanit & Chuensirimongkol 2015; Aktas, & Guven, 2015). There is evidence that suggests this transcendent goal is currently not accomplished due to a reliance on- traditional education approaches within the IB that miss the transcendent culture of ephemeral inspiration (Cole, et al., 2015; Grant, 2016).

The academic frame supporting this relationship lies in the core curriculum of the IB DP

— *The Theory of Knowledge* (TOK) (Haydorn & Jesudason, 2013). The IB DP brings forward

provoking questions through the TOK to put the IB DP gifted learner profile into practice

(Heydon & Jesudason, 2013). Supporting the IB DP TOK transcendent goal are numerous

studies regarding the IB overall obligation for out of the ordinary assistances among gifted

students (Jones & Hébert, 2012; Landis & Reschly, 2013; Preckel, Götz, & Frenzel, 2010; Vogl

& Preckel, 2014). Some researchers asked whether teachers challenge the needs of the gifted

and talented in a regular classroom (Benny & Blonder, 2016; Clickenbeard, 2016; Mathews,

2015). For example, Ozcan and Kotek (2015) conducted an empirical study with aim and

method requiring teachers to respond retrospectively about student reactions during the period of

being found as gifted. Beginning with teacher creativity, researchers sought to discover whether

there is a relationship between aesthetic curriculum and transactional experiences of students

(Fleet, 2007). These hypothetical inferences seek to find a worthwhile focus on the interaction

between student and teacher. Categorically, the encountered experiences between students and

teachers are an essential part of an evaluative study considering whether the IB reaches higher

sublimations of critical thought (Fleet, 2007). Different researchers have evaluated the IB for its

effects on the gifted students who were given the opportunity to experience the accelerated

learning curriculum (Culross & Tarver, 2011; Di Giorgio, 2010). For example, Culross and

Tarver (2011) found mixed effects in their 10-year study on the perspectives from an initial

group of IB students at the beginning of an IB program when compared to their perspectives

after they completed the program.

Within this associated research material, there is a knowledge base relating to the

interaction between student and teacher in the IB, and their associated influences going forward.

This study gauged that association using the authentic voice of students as they related to transactional outcomes, or transcendental thought, and higher order thinking.

Statement of the Problem

The enduring system of IB education represented as alternative education for gifted students is deficient in modes of learning, therefore, undermining the IB program's goal of producing critical and innovative thinkers (Smith & Morgan, 2010). One possible reason for this goal having not been successfully accomplished is a reliance on traditional education approaches that miss the transcendent culture of ephemeral inspiration (Cole, et al., 2015; Grant, 2016). Teachers have considerable influence over students, especially when academic station is in play (Stake & Munson, 2008). Like the matter-of-fact correlation between labor and management, the traditional arm's length relationship between teacher and student constitutes a barrier that may be too difficult a threshold to overcome (Marchand, Nardi, Reynolds, & Pamoukov, 2014). Even though IB is a respected program for gifted students worldwide, there are circumstances where gifted students do not reach the full potential of the IB education mandate: "To develop to their fullest potential the powers of each individual to understand, to modify and to enjoy his or her environment, both inner and outer, in its physical, social, moral, aesthetic, and spiritual aspects" (Peterson, 1987, p. 33). In addition, while IB students, as a group, meet an expectation of better academic performance, some IB students are constrained from the full scholastic potential of the IB (Cole, Ullman, Gannon, & Rooney, 2015). IB teaching professionals should be able to identify the ontological reality associated with IB students so compromising issues do not lead to uninspiring performance (Stake & Munson, 2008). Therefore, if not addressed, the dichotomy between theory and practice in the IB course management system may continue, and consequently marginalize the academic worth of the IB.

Purpose of the Study

The purpose of this qualitative phenomenological research study was to understand the lived experience of IB students and why higher order thinking may not be achieved within the IB. Qualitative research methods that focus on phenomenology are the best way to consider the IB derivation of knowledge because qualitative reports give rich descriptions of interrelated environments which can be accompanied by interpretations of influences and how they are felt (Moustakas, 1995). Grand collections of expressions work well when seen through the lens of experience based methodology (Katz, 2015).

The sample in this study was appropriate to the qualitative phenomenology norm of saturation coming from deep examination of the few (Moustakas, 1994). The research sample was used to explore the phenomenological experiences of five high school IB graduates who were exposed to IB prescriptive pedagogy. Teaching styles were discussed to explore the phenomenological experiences. Using In Vivo assessment developed by Charmaz, 2006; Corbin & Strauss, 2008; Glaser, 1978; Glaser & Strauss, 1967; Strauss, 1987; Strauss & Corbin, 1998, the researcher will sought to provide appraisal of student understandings of IB education from the qualitative perspective as first-hand, true-to-life, and systematic interpretations. The aggraded experience of student voices, may serve to deepen administrator and faculty introspection, potentially leading to curative measures.

Theoretical Framework Overview

The framework for this study bracketed two theoretical orders of social anthropology effecting the perception of the IB; Empirical Phenomenology (EP) and Transcendental Phenomenology (TP; Kordeš, 2016). However, these two theoretical classifications are subject to the administrative reach of science scholarship that identifies phenomenologists as journalists

5

or "soft" scientists (Lather, 2007). Qualitative researchers trying to understand the nature of lived experience are considered unable to find true statements in "voices from nowhere" (i.e., the inability or refusal of hard scientists to accept that something ethereal is true or real; Denzin & Lincoln, 2011, p. 123). For example, in quantum theory, Schrodinger's cats continue to be alive and dead at the same time (Crease & Goldhaber, 2014). This is a difficult position to understand among the realities of hard science.

These positions introduce the probability of hegemony among the modern archetypes of social science research. There is hope, albeit unlikely, that a resolution can blunt the rancorous pronouncements coming from both sides (Denzin & Lincoln, 2011). With this prospect in mind, regardless of unpleasant ruminations from meticulous intelligentsia, the frame of this study aggregated personal voice authenticities of students regarding their IB academic experience. In a general sense, one cannot expect findings within the frame of this study to change the political landscape of hard and soft science. Preferably, the split theoretical framework of this analysis may provide a glimpse into the future, such that humans may be entering an age of greater spirituality, the better angels of their nature, and this emerging transcendental spiritualism may be gaining traction among educators (Pinker, 2011).

Research Question

There was one research question for this study that deals with the lived experience of students associated with an IB program. The question is reflective because the students were graduates from the program, and answered as a retrospective. There were 22 principal questions designed to expand the development of the research questions from the student sample.

Research Question 1. What are IB students' lived experiences regarding the transactional and transcendental/transpersonal synthesizing of their critical skills leading to higher order thinking during, and after graduating from, the IB Diploma Program?

Nature of the Study

The character of this study was to to aggregate the perceptions, through authentic voice, of students in a regional U.S.A., IB program. Creswell (2014) suggested that inquiry-method studies lend themselves to qualitative interpretation. It is this qualitative interpretation that hallmarked the in-depth nature of this study's embedded design. Moustakas (1994) makes it clear that phenomenological research and design are best suited to individual in-depth inquiry. In this study a qualitative approach using student voice was used to support researcher interpretations of the student observations within the IB environment.

Cross, Stewart and Coleman (2011) developed a summary of research associated with the IB DP providing perspectives of students in the IB DP domain. There is an implied research assumption in phenomenology that individual contexts can be developed through inquiry to considerable depth (Coleman, Micko & Cross, 2015). It is consequently with little equivocation that Moustakas (1994) indicates phenomenological research and design represent "the building blocks of human science and the basis of all knowledge" (p. 26). The assumption, then, is that the learner profiles, combined with their expectations, will bring to bear the practice of the IB (Chatlos, 2015).

Sample size in qualitative research is from time to time associated with data saturation among a few rather than broad sample distribution curves among the many (Denzin & Lincoln, 2011). The sample in this study was appropriate to the qualitative phenomenology norm of saturation coming from deep examination of the few (Moustakas, 1994). To underwrite deep examination, the participants in this study were selected because of their dynamism in the IB. This academic spirit and energy was further supported by markers of being *gifted* for the student subjects. The selection method aligns with the study's purpose and research questions by its delimitation set for the participants as described in Chapter 3. These study parameters can be portrayed as a form of gerrymander toward having the researcher *look and look again.* The design steps ladder through inquiry-method redirections of motives, values, beliefs, and attitudes brought forward through student voice. The interview guide works within the frame of 22 key questions (see Appendix A) designed to focus the participant's self-examination toward a scaffolding of insights associated with the IB and the influences thereto going forward.

Significance of the Study

The study narrative operated in concert with established literature regarding gifted students (Swan et al., 2015). Gifted students deserve assurances that they will have access to cultivated professional understanding within the academic frame of advanced education in the IB (Baudson & Preckel, 2013; Cross et al., 2010; Geake & Gross, 2008). Around a significant broadening in classifications Cooper (1995) found "gifted students come from a wide variety of backgrounds with real IQ's ranging from the 85th to the 99th percentiles" (p. 10). This is a noteworthy range of measurable opportunity whose outliers may be overlooked by teachers, further leading to a problematic correct identification of students with high critical thinking potential because of an analytic dependency upon standardized instruments (Cooper, 1995). Intelligence Quotient testing notwithstanding, this study moved outside analytics to an inquiry-based method of meaningful thought about the impact of the IB in-place advanced academic system.

This study was significant by its approach to the transcendent quality of student voice. To find embedded opportunities for transcendence going beyond the transactional exchange of ordinary education, participants were taken to their full potential of reflective thought (Beavan, 2011). This method comes with narrative collaboration in its significance of whether teachers, in fact, challenge the needs of exceptional students (Benny & Blonder, 2016; Clickenbeard, 2016; Mathews, 2015).

Through allowing this study's participants to express their *voice* in the deepest terms of transactional and transcendental learning, this research formed a weighbridge for IB Beta Test incubation (Abadzi, Martelli, & Primativo, 2014). By adding to the knowledge base of advanced education opportunities, this analysis had direct inferences on methodology used to identify and advance higher order thinking among gifted students.

Definition of Key Terms

Being and Time. Being and Time are separate, one-to-the-other. Heidegger believed being is time. That is, what it means for a human being to be is to exist temporally in time. They are impossible to marry together in space. They both change in relation to each other and not in relation to each other, however not synchronously (Heidegger, 1919/1920).

Cognitive skill. Cognitive skill is the ability to discuss new information in one's own words (Granena, 2016).

Constructivism. Constructivism is a learning approach bridging social integration and thought where learning is based on mental construction of knowledge (Vall Castelló, 2016). Mentally constructed understandings that reflect personal experiences become mental models of actualities (Juvova, Chudy, Neumeister, Plischke, & Kvintova, 2015).

Critical Thinking. Critical thinking is laboring toward the composition of deep thought; seeing things framed as an intellectually disciplined moment in conceptualization and evaluation (NCECT, 1987; Tarhan, 2015).

Empirical Phenomenology. Empirical Phenomenology is the research process analytically separated into steps reflecting a transactional retrospective of reality, becoming iterations between potential meanings establishing prospective (Husserl, 2002/1931).

Epoche. Epoche is the accumulation of data that requires the elimination of suppositions and the rising of knowledge at every permutation (Moustakas, 1995).

Gestalt. Gestalt is like synergism as something that is made of many parts while in being is more or different from the combination of its parts (Ponte, 2014/1945).

Gifted Student. As an aggregation of the attempts, a gifted student is one who demonstrates intellectual high performance (Bahadır, 2016). There is no universally accepted definition of giftedness; however, there are 400 attempts on record with SAGE (Kerr, 2009).

Intentionality. Intentionality is the power of one's mind to accommodate positions on things, properties and states of affairs. Of being directed towards some goal or thing in suspension away from being and time (Heidegger, 1919/1920).

Phaenesthai. Phaenesthai and phenomena enjoy the same meaning among human tribes. The use *phaenesthai* is to use the Greek phaenesthai phenomenon of phaenesthai - to flare up only to appear passive (Heidegger, 2013/1962).

Phenomenology. Phenomenology is a science movement dealing with the abstraction of existence. In this discipline, object awareness is an intellection of reality (Julmi & Scherm, 2015).

Quantum mechanics. Quantum Mechanics is/are aggregated through a mathematical description of the motion and interaction of subatomic particles. Quantum mechanics is the phenomena that does not fit in the elegant world of Newtonian science. A chink in the armor of prior assumptions about space, time, and causality incorporating the concepts of wave-particle duality (Crease & Goldhaber, 2014).

Structuralism. Structuralism is a method of interpretation and analysis of human cognition that focuses on human trait underlying a superficial diversity (Heinz-Jurgen & Schmidt, 2014). In phenomenology, the claim that structure is more important than function (Kwan & Wong, 2015).

Transcendental phenomenology. Transcendental phenomenology is the reasoning claim that a sub-conclusion or conclusion is a presupposition and necessary condition of a premise. That priori concepts through evolutionary process apply to intentions playing a part in our experience (Moustakas, 1995).

Transpersonal phenomenology. Transpersonal phenomenology is the direct experience of a sudden awakening without regard for analyticity or intentions (Ponte, 2014/1945)

Summary

The development of the IB as an educational service on the road to higher-order thinking continues as a burgeoning discipline with a possibility of transcendental experiences (Budsankom, Sawangboon, Damrongpanit & Chuensirimongkol 2015; Aktas, & Guven, 2015). The growth of the IB finds its heritage in the prescience of John Dewey 1895-1952, A.S. Smith 1883-1973, Jean Piaget 1896-1980, and Jerome Bruner 1915 – present (International Baccalaureate, 2016). Coalescing the views of these thinkers was Robert Leach, as the original promoter of the International Baccalaureate (IB), who took the IB concept forward by organizing the Conference of Internationally-minded Schools (International Baccalaureate, 2016). As an agreed upon naming convention the conference participants recommended the program be known as "International Baccalaureate."

The IB evolved as a not-for-profit organization with its focus on cross-disciplinary education, thereby encouraging students across the world to become active lifelong learners (Park, Caine & Wimmer, 2014). The global reach of the IB finds its way into many levels of literature (Corlu, 2014; Fitzgerald, 2015; Jamal, 2016; Kadıoğlu, & Erişen, 2016). However, Tarc and Beatty (2012) found IB programs routinely fail to deliver an education outcome beyond the scaled rubric of quantitative prescription (Tarc & Beatty, 2012). Among possible reasons for this target shortfall is a dependence on conventional education approaches that avoid transcendent hyper stimulation (Cole, et al., 2015; Grant, 2016). Moreover, while IB students, as an education segment, meet a general expectancy of improved academic accomplishment, some IB students seem to miss the maximum IB instructional possibility of the IB (Cole, Ullman, Gannon, & Rooney, 2015). Consequently, the contradiction between theory and practice in the IB may be better realized through academic research.

Recognizing the need for additional research this study went deep into the IB environment using student voice. The voice of qualitative inquiry provides breadth and scope to experienced centered approaches (Katz, 2015). These descriptions, accompanied by interpretations, became the matrix of this study (Moustakas, 1995). Supporting the study's format is substantial research indicating the findings and interpretations 'accord the study a character of deep introspection by using In Vivo assessment. The root meaning of In Vivo which is "in that which is alive" highlights the research questions in such a way that researchers can expect expanded practitioner adoption going forward (Strauss, 1987).

Chapter 2: Literature Review

This study put forward a qualitative phenomenological examination of the lived experience of students set apart as a cohort in the IB DP. The literature inquiry combines knowledge areas beginning with overlays of the 20th Century existential thinkers of Europe. This is followed by extensively analyzed modern education theorists formulating their ideas and guidelines in explaining learning behavior associated with critical thinking and its involvement in the potential phenomenology of higher order thinking within the IB DP. The review became specific to the socialization of gifted students, and student relationships with various stakeholders in the education community. This education community investigation runs analogous with an examination of family culture when a household recognizes a member as being gifted. Finally, using additional IB research, the literature review drew demographic examples of how the IB does, or does not, meet established goals in market segments both foreign and domestic. From the aggregated assessments, perspectives arose from the literature regarding the prescriptive frequency of critical thinking tenures in secondary education. Investigation emerged regarding whether teachers recognize gifted students when using a reliance on Intelligent Quotient IQ testing available to the discovery process. The flaws of IQ testing became apparent when measured among ethnic groups, where perceptions vary regarding who is, and who is not, gifted. These examinations were, then, related back to the IB DP for their outward appearance of expectations. Ahead of presenting the literature review, documentation indicates how the material in the literature was assembled.

Documentation

The review of literature includes four main sections.

Theoretical framework, the research on gifted students, the literature on the nature of critical thinking skills, and the research on IB. The academic documents used encompass book chapters, journal articles and dissertations are all reviewed. Keywords used to search academic libraries and Google Scholar, EBCOHost, and many more include critical thinking skills, gifted education, gifted students, international baccalaureate, international baccalaureate diploma program, international baccalaureate primary years program, international baccalaureate Middle Years Program (MYP), and international baccalaureate career-related program, and the effects of international baccalaureate program.

Theoretical Framework

Positivism has dominated social science research methods since the beginning of the 20th century. Positivists use this theoretical method to hold that rationally justifiable assertions can be systematically verified using logic or arithmetical proof, therefore rejecting metaphysics and theism, regardless of the rise of spiritualism (Hasan, 2016). Conversely, phenomenology consists of a move toward the study of consciousness that metaphorically uses a lens of absolute experience (Julmi & Scherm, 2015).

Both positivism and phenomenology have advantages one to the other. Empirically, positivists establish recognizable markers for focused research: Positivists use a kind of Newtonian approach (i.e., EP; Sanders, 2015). Conversely, unconfined phenomenology becomes a liberal expression of the empirical discipline by allowing the mind and spirit to misdirect from the common sense of normal logic (i.e., Transcendental Phenomenology; Brook, 2016). This transcendent, almost irresistible amplified version of sensation lends itself to the quantum side of social anthropology, where there becomes a complementary particle/wave

analogy for body and spirit (Crease & Goldhaber, 2014).

Within the complementary particle/wave theory likeness, researchers cited the formation

of the relationship between self-actualization and infinite human potential (Crease & Goldhaber,

2014). For example, both branches of knowledge are influenced by culture, socialization, and

history involving the freedoms of the human condition (Russell, 2013). However, this

problematic bilateral existence seems too difficult for unilateral thinkers. Some social scientists

truly feel that empirical examination stands steadfast against the unpredictability of the

transcendental nature of certain types of phenomenological experience (Nixon, 2016). The

contrast remains in the perceived flawed and compromising experiences of transcendentalism

that have juxtaposed to the highly specific detail of empirical examination. Empirical

stipulations are easier to understand and quantify.

Both theories are influenced by constructivism as a learning theory of created knowledge

(Chaipichit, Jantharajit, & Chookhampaeng, 2015). Constructivists created the assumption that

humans are engaged in the world without recourse (Juvova, Chudy, Neumeister, Plischke, &

Kvintova, 2015). No other option exists, but for one to remain present in thought and actuality

(Juvova et al., 2015). This seemingly empirical understanding stood opposed to the quantum

approach of dualism, allowing the mind and body to separate at different points in time

(Kinghorn, 2015).

In 1935, the EPR argument/Copenhagen interpretation occurred (as cited in Rosenblum

& Kuttner, 2011). All three scientists agreed to the paradox of divine action and scientific truth

in separate arguments. Rosenblum and Kuttner (2011) cited Albert Einstein, Boris Polaski, and

15

Nathan Rosen as stating that physical reality was not describable through particle or wave theory but rather the physical realities of each requiring additional study.

The hypothesis can be taken seriously that human bodies have the capacity to grasp the immediate gestalt of reality (Hatfield, 2014). The context could be described by two children looking at a field of grain

"Well, when we observe them, they become amber particles of grain" (Crease & Goldhaber, 2014, p. 111). Not unlike Merleau-Ponty's (1996) opinion from the Phenomenology of Perception, there is no need for structure. Perception is modified by the actuality, and perception is based on positioning. There is some humor here, as Merleau-Ponty (1996) appeared to explain the phenomenology of perception with Newtonian theory.

However, when the conversation moves to transcendental phenomenology, the lens is re-focused on Being and Time (Heidegger, 1962). This work contains implications of the sophistication of the human condition, which cannot be couched in specific ways to meet the analog requirements of mathematical inference of energy and mass. Transcendental phenomenology finds mastery in moving away from the normative (Doyon, 2016). In this case, humans create physical realities by observation and without any physical force (Husserl, 1931, 2002). This, seen from the human perspective, is quantum mechanics encountering consciousness (Doyon, 2016). One may question whether this concept represents the balance postulated by administrators of the IB. This will lead to more study. Like the Copenhagen agreement in 1945, social science mingles with the empiricism of biologic interpretation. Therefore, research of perception through empiricism and transcendentalism is "valid, one to the other, regardless of what hides in the physicist's closet" (Dyck, 2015, p. 9).

The goal of this theoretical framework is to provide an overarching intellectual scaffold to the theoretical prospect that EP may lead to TP among IB graduates. The theory ascending in this study was student voice elaborations of EP leading to TP among gifted students (Beavan, 2011). In deference to all of science, assumptions remained unilateral addressing issues each in its own way, avoiding the hubristic dichotomy of inter-institutional power.

Evidence from phenomenological investigations derives from the autobiographical meanings and values of the study sample (Adnrousopoulou, 2015). There emerged a research model which, through validation of data and review of professional research literature, contained a summary of implications and outcomes through a human resource side of phenomenological analysis (Adnrousopoulou, 2015). The transcendental phenomenology became a reflective meditation of determined self-presence that recognizes phaenesthai (i.e., flare-up) constructed in its intentionality as a phenomenon (Crease & Goldhaber, 2014; Heidegger, 1962, 2013; Moustakas, 1994). What is presented and what is imagined provides the basis of phenomenon. The transcendental nature of that phenomenon can present itself as an epiphany or a cognitive construction. However, regardless of the science mechanics, there always emerges a fascinating tour of life's alternatives in its most captivating moments.

Alternative Education for Gifted Students

The enduring system of International Baccalaureate (IB) program education, an alternative education for gifted students, is deficient in modes of learning, which undermines the IB program's goal of producing critical and innovative thinkers (Smith & Morgan, 2010). One possible reason for the unsuccessful implementation of this goal may derive from a reliance on traditional educators' approaches that miss the transcendent culture of ephemeral inspiration

(Cole, Ullman, Gannon, & Rooney, 2015; Grant, 2016). Teachers have considerable influence over students, especially when academic station occurs (Stake & Munson, 2008).

The traditional relationship between teacher and student constitutes a barrier that may be too difficult a threshold to overcome (Marchand, Nardi, Reynolds, & Pamoukov, 2014). Even though IB is a respected program for gifted students worldwide, circumstances remain where gifted students do not reach the full potential of the IB education mandate: "To develop to their fullest potential the powers of each individual to understand, to modify and to enjoy his or her environment, both inner and outer, in its physical, social, moral, aesthetic, and spiritual aspects" (Peterson, 2003, p. 33). In addition, while IB students, as a group, meet an expectation of better academic performance, some IB students are constrained from the full scholastic potential of the IB (Cole et al., 2015). IB teaching professionals should identify the ontological reality associated with IB students to avoid compromising issues that lead to uninspiring performance (Stake & Munson, 2008). Therefore, the dichotomy between theory and practice in the IB course management system may be better understood through additional study.

The purpose of this phenomenological research study was to understand the nuances of transcendental education and why higher order thinking was not being achieved within the IB. Qualitative research methods that focus on phenomenology were the best way to consider the IB derivation of knowledge because qualitative reports give rich descriptions of interrelated environments; these are accompanied by interpretations of influences (Moustakas, 1995). Grand collections of expressions work well when seen through the lens of experience based methodology.

The Evolution of Transcendental Phenomenology

Husserl (1931) interpreted meanings and essences considering intuitive reflections as they appear. However, Husserl (1931) had to blend the imagined and the real from his vantage point of possible meanings. This brought the co-mingling of real and ideal by marking "the core difference between strictly phenomenological and, on the other hand, aesthetic experience" (Lanier, 2015, p. 186). In this circumstance, the object that appears in consciousness intermingles with an object in nature to create a meaning, and knowledge is extended (Blau, Bach, Scott, Rubin, & Clark, 2013). Therefore, Husserl (1931, 2002) wanted to find the intent by studying merged perception and reality. He referred to this as "intentionality" (Moustakas, 1994, p. 28). From Husserl's (1931, 2002) synthesis came the refined belief that nature maintains a consistent presentation while human consciousness operates in variations. Armed with these notions, Max Plank, Niels Bohr, and others brought science to the threshold of quantum mechanics (as cited by Crease & Goldhaber, 2014). Consequently, these descriptions by mid-20th Century existential phenomenologists remained open to interpretation (Crease & Goldhaber, 2014).

Following Husserl (1931), Heidegger (1962) expanded the interpretation by focusing on the appearance of truth (i.e., that perception of truth views and shapes all aspects of our being in the world; Lanier, 2015). Heidegger (1969) capitalized the adjective Being, giving it the power to work as the fundamental definition of everything that exists. In short, Being comes ahead of essence; therefore, without Being there can be no essence or perception (Heidegger, 1962, 2013). Traditional scholarship's emphasis is on what is (Lahman et al., 2015). Heidegger observed that it might be revealing to study what is not (Heidegger, 2013, p. 121-123). Therefore, Heidegger (1962) took Husserl's (1931) seeing things as reality and rested that theory on his philosophy of

Being as the fundamental notion of truth. Being then became the infinite project without the definite endpoint. Being was everything in the past and the future. By using Being as his platform, Heidegger (1962) expanded on Husserl's (1931) philosophy by combining nature and perception into actuality. Heidegger (1962) speculated that it is philosophically correct to say that sophisticated individuals could be ruled by inauthenticity and unsophisticated persons could live in a most authentic way following their own devices (Heidegger, 1962, p. 25).

With Husserl (1931) and Heidegger (1962) laying the groundwork for existential philosophy in Germany, Merleau-Ponty (1996) turned Heidegger's (1962) work into a conversation about skill and perception. Merleau-Ponty (1996) wanted to know how one would respond to a specific state of play. Anxiety and risk do not interest Merleau-Ponty (1996). Instead, this author focused on ways in which humans' cope with situations. For example, how does a person become an expert and respond to a situation? From Merleau-Ponty's (1996) stance, human bodies have the capacity to grasp and imitate Gestalt of what is going on. There is no need for structure (Merleau-Ponty, 1996).

Merleau-Ponty (1996) pursued how one defined and understood reality. In Merleau-Ponty's (1996) perception of how one sees things, the perception is modified by the actuality. Circumstances or items seen from one perspective can be completely different from another perspective. An example would be viewing a tavern façade on a movie set. At what degree-of-angle does the observer realize that there is no more to the tavern than the facade? Or, at what distance from earth does one realize there is life on the planet? Merleau-Ponty (1996) believed that human bodies are moved in perception to an optimal position. People somehow know where the optimal positioning resides. When a person perceives an object, the object leads the person's mind to examine the object from multiple angles. This perception or phenomenon of perception does not require structure. This perception is automatic and embedded in humans as a species (Marshall, 2008). Merleau-Ponty (1996) was the first philosopher to recognize the relationship between man and object as a matter of perception. Diprose and Reynolds (2014), examining Merleau-Ponty's (1996) work, found the following:

> While phenomenology is the study of essences, including the essence of perception, or the essence of consciousness, phenomenology also puts essences back into existence, and does not expect to arrive at an understanding of man and the world from any starting point other than that of their facticity. (p. 10)

Expanding his reach in similarity with original thinkers, Merleau-Ponty (1996) saw this process as shared mastery. Merleau-Ponty (1996) took Heidegger's (1962) concept of where people are in space and time, and extended it to perception of every day events. His conception was more practical and less ethereal. Heidegger (1962) laid the foundation for Merleau-Ponty (2014), leading one to realize that the possibility of masterful wisdom exists; moreover, with that wisdom, one can use practical perception to think critically of the world. For Merleau-Ponty (2014), perception owes nothing to what one would otherwise know about the world. For Merleau-Ponty (2014), perception is not present as a "category of causality but rather a reconstruction of the world at that moment" (p. 251).

Critical Thinking

As an evolutionary byproduct of existential thought, affirming or implying the existence of a thing, critical thinking (CT) endures in the same tradition of being unclear to/and by an undecided social science community (The National Council for Excellence in Critical Thinking, 2016). This notwithstanding, while evolving over two millennia, the connection between Aristotle and mid-20th century existential philosophy and contemporary critical thinking remain aligned (Brogan, 2005). For example, looking to its historical discussion, within his existential preview of Aristotelian philosophy, Heidegger (2013) relied on Aristotle's blatant first passages where Aristotle made a distinction between "vocal announcements" and "thinking" by contrasting the communication orders of animals and humans (Wu, 2015, p. 268).

In this contrasting order, critical thinking is, in fact, about thinking. The originators of organized thought (i.e., Aristotle, Plato, and Socrates) remained in the ethereal school of thinking rather than doing (Mintz & Tal, 2014). German and French protagonists, Husserl (1931, 2002), Heidegger (1996, 2013), and Morleau-Ponty's (1962, 2014) interpretations brought thinking forward as a holistic approach to perception; furthermore, perception prevailed as the best identifier for thinking critically about the world (Husserl, 1931, 2002). Perception became respected as part of social science, and critical thinking became normative and identified as prescriptive or descriptive in academic environments (Polowczyk, 2013). Normalization, in every culture, evolves through agency intervention (Woelders & Abma, 2015). Therefore, in the United States, society has the National Council for Excellence in Critical Thinking (2016), which defines critical thinking as follows:

> Critical thinking is the intellectually disciplined process of actively and skillfully conceptualizing, applying, analyzing, synthesizing, and/or evaluating information gathered from, or generated by, observation, experience, reflection, reasoning, or communication, as a guide to belief and action. In its exemplary form, it is based on universal intellectual values that transcend subject matter divisions: clarity, accuracy, precision, consistency, relevance, sound evidence, good reasons, depth, breath, and fairness (para. 2).

The process endures that strong critical thinking outcomes require scaffolding of method (Jordan & Lande, 2016). These processes include planning, execution, and suitable content that allows explicit outcomes (Heinrich, Habron, Johnson, & Goralnik, 2015). Juxtaposed to this prescriptive method are educators securing conclusions that one cannot find critical thinking without entering the ethereal realm of abstraction (Richards, 2015).

Knowles et al. (2014) showed critical thinking in a structural area of the IB for the reason that the IB Diploma Program (DP) is split by the accepted age transition between pedagogy and andragogy. However, while the IB DP is creating learners during a critical period, ages 16 through 19, educators are doing so without a stated regard for the transition from pedagogy to andragogy (Park, Caine, & Wimmer, 2014). Student cohorts in the IB DP are transitioning from learning through pedagogy as adolescents and moving toward learning through andragogy toward adulthood. The learning process of these two groups is different, and change is expected to occur.

In the pedagogical model, the teacher is responsible for the entire learning event (Knowles et al., 2014, p. 60). The andragogic model is based on a student's need to know (Knowles et al., 2014, p. 63). Amplifying Knowles et al. (2014) and the actuality of this CT transition from pedagogy to andragogy, Fornaciari and Dean (2014) contended that although literature shows support for advances in learning technology, development of the syllabus as a well-established functioning explanatory learning tool appears to have been left out of the evolving conversation. Other researchers, specific to the IB DP, discuss the potential absence of syllabus related dialogue during the transition from pedagogy to andragogy (Cole et al., 2015; Grant, 2016).

In 2002, Daniel Kahneman won the Nobel Prize in Economic Sciences for his pioneering work with Amos Tversky in the critical aspects of thinking fast and thinking slow (as cited by Polowczyk, 2013). Kahneman (2011) stated that intuitive thinking was fast and deliberative thinking was slow (O'Brien, 2012). Kahneman's (2011) research showed support that intuition becomes a reflection of pedagogy and deliberative thinking becomes a reflection of andragogy. Within pedagogy, there is an illusion of confidence; for example, even if people's beliefs are preposterous, these are also essential to form human growth through the middle teen years. Andragogy represents the reverse, where the illusion drops away, causing a person to look for possible antecedents toward a deeper understanding of particular circumstances (Knowles et al., 2014).

Kahneman (2011) provided an unintended accretion for research regarding relationships between empirical and transcendental phenomenology. The applications to education that rest between empirical studies with foundations in hard science and phenomenological studies with foundations in transcendentalism (soft science) maintain a common thread through much of the research (Rosenblum & Kuttner, 2011; Maggini, 2013).

There are also applications for mixed methods in similar research. For example, Akmansoy and Kartal (2014) completed an empirical quantitative study using 30 experienced faculty members who understood qualitative methods. The researchers used a rubric as part of its conceptual framework to track internal validity. The researchers relied on binomial outcomes, comparing these with applications of chaos theory to see if the researchers could replicate the effect of one to the other, ending with an 86.7% continuity finding among members of the sample. Therefore, there seemed an interest in all categories of scientific research, especially if the Akmansoy and Kartal's (2014) study is a trending indication.

Some challengers of the orthodoxy of cognitive phenomenology exist. Within the last 5 years, several studies involving perceptual experience have surfaced. For example, Bayne and Montague (2011) stated that the meanings of phenomenology derived from nomenclatures of logic and cognition. The researches took a principle step toward cognitive phenomenology and arguments on reflection. Therefore, once again, the literature reverted to the original phenomenological thinkers, with a focus on the descriptive experience of seeing things as they are in the classic Husserl (1931, 2002) context.

Bringing things as they are in a parallel context forward, and refining the possibility to the specific parameters of this study, an overarching leap of emphasis on discussions regarding gifted learners existed. This progression advanced toward cognitive expression, as described in various ways, including empirical and transcendental phenomenology (Grañena, 2016). Current researchers have tried to cross the symbolic threshold toward quantum mechanics in relation to understanding themselves as observers or participants in a transactional or transcendental process (Crease & Goldhaber, 2014). This current inclination, working analogous with phenomenological philosophy, takes a parallel path forward in light of Einstein, Podolsk, and Rosen's 1935 decision to agree that there is an enigma in matters seen and unseen that are not observable, acting simultaneously as a quantum entanglement (as cited by Crease & Goldhaber, 2014).

The definition of critical thinking over history has changed as new schools of thought provide new insights and knowledge bases that redefine out of date lines of reasoning. Because of this, the concept of logical or critical thinking will again change in the future as new ideas are presented. Critical thinking has and will therefore continue to evolve with time. With this insight, the question includes whether people will continue to evolve and live in harmony with nature.

Student and Teacher

Thomas (2011) explained that well-educated students could utilize critical thinking skills in order to (a) make "well-informed judgments," (b) explain their "reasoning" when they arrive at required answers, and (c) be able to arrive at solutions to "unknown problems" (p. 26). Each individual instructor should take time in his or her classroom to provide explicit instructions (and training), regarding critical thinking strategies and skills. However, Thomas (2011) insisted that educators should teach freshmen (first year students) these important skills to "cope with their future studies" and evaluate issues once in the workforce (Thomas, 2011).

For one thing, using critical thinking skills in the first year empowers students to continue learning about and using critical thinking skills through the next three years of university life. Further, whether it is history or economics, critical thinking skills transcend specific areas of study; critical thinking skills should be thought of as tools to aid students in understanding the narratives provided in difficult textbooks as well as the scholarly articles they are required to read and digest as part of important assignments. As forks and spoons are tools for eating, critical thinking skills are tools for comprehension and problem-solving (Thomas, 2011).

Should critical thinking skills be taught as a separate course of study, or should these skills be integrated into the specific discipline area? If the skills are to be taught as "complimentary" to another subject, then the authors suggested that educators should teach critical thinking skills independently. Conversely, if one employs critical thinking skills to "translate" important concepts, then Thomas (2011) suggested these important skills should derive from any discipline that educators presented to students (p. 27).

In a helpful list of the various critical thinking skills, Thomas presented the many dimensions that critical thinking skills present: (a) evaluating "different points of view," (b) open-mindedness and the development of "a logical argument with appropriate evidence," (c) zeroing in on weaknesses and strengths of arguments, (d) identifying "bias in themselves and others," (e) providing analysis and synthesis of myriad sources, (f) applying deductive and inductive reasoning directed toward a specific topic, (g) solving problems and developing additional criteria for evaluation, (h) evaluating one's work and decision-making processes, and (i) using reflective judgment and "self-regulation" (Thomas, 2011, p. 28).

Thomas (2011) also provided four helpful methods for instructors that contain worthy instruction of critical thinking skills to students. Method 1 involves asking a student to evaluate the quality of sources to be found in the Internet. This should entail a simple exercise for students because the great majority of students use the Internet daily. Thomas (2011) provided six bullet points to guide students as they surf the World Wide Web (e.g., questions pertaining to the validity of the site, the intended audience, the source of the information, etc.).

The second method is the "analysis of an argument," which breaks the students into small groups (2 to 4 people per group) and gives them projects to complete involving the investigation of materials found in books and online. The purpose included (a) to "help them learn to analyze arguments and how to combine different people's ideas into one piece of work," (b) to help them explain the reasoning to others, and (c) to help them learn to reference properly (Thomas, 2011, p. 26).

The third method is to develop critical thinking and logical thinking using the technique called "immediate feedback assessment technique" (Thomas, 2011, p. 26). This entailed a process in which students work in a group and answer questions in a multiple-choice test. They do it individually and after all have finished, they compare answers and come up with a consensus as the correct answer. According to Thomas (2011), this gives students practice at defending their own reasoning. The questions may be considered right or wrong, which depends on a person's perspective. Lastly, a good method included using rubrics and reflection as a means of self-regulation. Students learn critical thinking by evaluating themselves through different criteria presented by the instructor. Through self-evaluation, students build knowledge of criteria that an instructor presented for an assignment, and they can more fully understand what the instructor expects in terms of getting a good grade in the class (Thomas, 2011).

Researchers suspected that many students do not understand critical thinking. Some think that "critical thinking" involves being "critical" about a given topic (Bensley et al., 2016; Moore, 2013). This of course is not true, and it is an echo of another misunderstanding of the words critical and "criticism." When a scholar reviews an opera or a movie in detail, digging into the style and substance of a performance, his or her work is called criticism and he/she are known as "critics." But a critic may love a certain film after critically evaluating it in the contest of popular movies. Again, critically evaluating a film or opera may result in a positive position by the critic. To wit the understood moral imperative of the unbiased nature of research.

Gifted Students

A gifted student is one who demonstrates intellectually high performance (Bahadır, 2016). Gifted students are described in many ways, with no universally accepted definition of giftedness; however, 400 attempts exist on record with SAGE (Kerr, 2009). With 400 attempts of record, identifying students as gifted becomes a Sisyphean task. Although giftedness is un-mandated by the U.S. government, there are two organizations within government that introduce the definition. First, from the National Association of Gifted Children (NAGC; 2016), "Gifted individuals are those who demonstrate outstanding levels of aptitude or competence in one or more domains. Domains include any structured area of activity with its own symbol system and/or set of sensorimotor skills" (para. 1).

In addition, the federal definition stated

> The term the gifted and talented when used with respect to students, children, or youth, means students, children, or youth who give evidence of high achievement capability in areas such as intellectual, creative, artistic, or leadership capacity, or in specific academic fields, and who need services or activities not ordinarily provided by the school in order to develop those capabilities. (No Child Left Behind Act, 2002)

Among all definitions, gifted students are sometimes categorized as "twice exceptional" which, in this study's context, means a potential for high achievement in more than one domain, as opposed to the conventional definition of being gifted while comingled with a learning disability (Reis, Baum, & Burke, 2014, p. 217). This researcher used gifted students as an assimilation of all categories, leaving additional refinements for further study.

In the education domain, gifted students demonstrate realized learning gains from the scaffolding associated with complex, advanced, and meaningful content, provided by equally disciplined teachers (Siegle et al., 2016). Conversely, gifted students tend not to be recognized unless there are existing opportunities that engage their emerging talent. If recognized, this emergence begins the scholarly process to exceptional levels (Siegle et al., 2016). Because there is no federal mandate identifying gifted as a student category, there are many applications to giftedness servicing their own guidelines; therefore, student growth represents a preview of policymakers within relatively small communities of stakeholders nationwide (Siegle et al., 2016). This makes the ratification process difficult to assess through forms of policy coagulation. Effectively, teachers, parents, and other interested stakeholders become talent

scouts operating on intuition. Through this process, some educators fear multiple bifurcations

among students causing some to feel inferior if gifted students are identified (Plunkett &

Kronborg, 2011). However, as the federal definition implies, there are numerous studies

supporting the requirement for special services among gifted students (Jones & Hébert, 2012;

Landis & Reschly, 2013; Preckel, Götz, & Frenzel, 2010; Vogl & Preckel, 2014). The

unintended consequences of pressure from all sides leads the public school system to look to the

government for ratification of fitness based on minimum competency for the greater good of all

(Cross, Cross, & Finch, 2010, p. 246).

This wide-open, albeit narrow, restriction creates an inverse proportion of underserved

students who may be gifted (Gentry, Hu, & Thomas, 2008). Programs, designed to identify

academic skills, are necessary to develop future talents and varied with students of privilege

enjoying a competitive edge (Gentry et al., 2008). Historically the benchmark for intelligence is

the ubiquitous IQ test and standardized test scores (Richardson & Norgate, 2015). More

recently, identification methods have expanded to include the ethereal power of intuition;

however, these contain empirical assessments through reviewed work and third-party

recommendations (Richardson & Norgate, 2015).

One must note that some of the disaggregated statistics show gifted student's

relationships in the overall U.S. population. Among K-12 students studied in calendar years,

2011 and 2012, underserved categories exist who continue to struggle for recognition. For

example, during those calendar years, 4% of African-American and Black student populations

were considered gifted compared to 8% of White students. In schools where gifted students

were formed in cohorts, 57% of African-American students were considered having high potential compared to 81% of White students experiencing the same consideration (U.S. Department of Education Office for Civil Rights, 2014). These metrics represent a societal distortion, suggesting the need for an inclusive system of gifted student identification. Considering a universal consensus on gifted identification and outcomes does not exist; the multiple views available to this research from the study sample will be reflective on the anomalous, as well as the customary.

Being Gifted

An area of ongoing concern within academic literature is gifted student peer pressure. Vanderbrook (2006) suggested that gifted students do not associate the challenges of advanced academic programs to their faculty. Instead, student challenges are related to their peer relationships and pressures associated with day-to-day success. Vanderbrook (2006) conducted a phenomenological study asking for students lived experiences and the meaning of that experience. The conclusions showed that all the participants encountered peer pressure challenges and became psychologically unstable in some cases; however, faculty members or administrators were not considered a problem. From this literature, the consensus emerges that faculty and staff receive remedial training in how to deal with peer pressure among students (Vanderbrook, 2006).

Wintergerst, DeCapua, and Verna, (2003) summarized the cause of peer pressure among gifted students as an "unestablished intellectual compatibility among cohorts" (p. 98). Other students expressed difficulty with assimilation; as Donovan and Cross (2002) identified, the greater risk of alienation due to unestablished intellectual compatibility might create underachievement among the potentially gifted students. These outcomes seem to ratify the ongoing assumptions that a consensus on academic outcomes is being continually subverted by the socialization process among student populations and that a general understanding of these causes is difficult to achieve across a broad cross- section of student populaces.

Perceptions of Gifted Students

People who demonstrate intellectual high performance comprise approximately 2% of society (Gökdere, Küçük, & Çepni, 2003). Servicing that 2% are teachers and parents, considered stakeholders. Stakeholders, who do not receive additional help regarding the characteristics of giftedness, are likely to hold hegemonic misconceptions about students who may be perceived as having a disability as opposed to a gift (Baudson & Preckel, 2013; Plunkett & Kronborg, 2011). Gökdere et al. (2003) indicated teachers in favor of special services for gifted students, as well as teachers against such services, hold subliminally negative attitudes toward students with higher order tendencies (Baudson & Preckel, 2013; Cross et al., 2010; Geake & Gross, 2008). The researchers found that gifted student stakeholders might "view these potential higher orders of consciousness as [a] form of ethereal metaphysics not acceptable to the common man" (Baudson & Preckel, 2013, p. 37).

Therefore, a common thread from parents and teachers of gifted students included a need for increased education to help cope with the demand of the intellectual high performance from their custodies. Parents and teachers learned that attaining situational consciousness represented a hallmark of people associated with the gifted (Jedlikowska, 2014). Developmentally, it is necessary that parents and teachers are not neglected as part of the progressive scaffolding that moves along the gifted learner's intellectual continuum (Butvilas, 2014). This parent/teacher education, to be effective, must mirror their student/s acquiring interest and capacity (Davasligil, 2000). Determining the educational needs of both parents, teachers, and gifted students may come close to finalizing a consensus on a definition of gifted as more of a communal project that enlists at least three fully engaged stakeholders for each student demonstrating intellectual high performance.

Taxonomy

It is a natural state of fact today that schools, which exclusively serve the needs of the blind, are widely available. Likewise, it is rare today for a public school not to devote classroom space and educational resources toward the heightened needs of special education students. These are facts that, rather than subverting the democratic values of public education, enhance its ability to serve the needs of all students, regardless of what must be acknowledged as differences. The students were offered the facilities, resources, and attention demanded by their respectively specialized needs; hence, they were better equipped to realize their fullest opportunity for educational growth (Gökdere et al., 2003). There is a direct parallel to these practical distinctions in the experience of the so-called gifted child. Gifted children can be identified as those who "learn new material in much less time. . . tend to remember forever what they already have learned and . . .they perceive ideas and concepts at more abstract and complex levels than other students their age" (Winebrenner, 1999, p. 14).

While it has become socially unpopular and to some extent diminished by educational philosophers who have derided such principles as promoting elitism and social divisions, the distinguishing of gifted students from the general population is crucial to their educational growth. Some researchers have determined whether these needs are being met in general educational contexts (Baudson & Preckel, 2013; Cross et al., 2010; Geake & Gross, 2008). There is little question that some students rise above the others in terms of ability. Eventually, if their talents are cultivated properly, today's students will become the *movers and shakers* of our world. They do what others only talk about doing. Bright and talented persons frequently become the creative producers on whom society depend for technological innovations.

Some researchers asked whether teachers challenge the needs of the gifted and talented in a regular classroom (Benny & Blonder, 2016; Clickenbeard, 2016; Mathews, 2015). To address this question, the research process will often be guided by several subsidiary questions that revolve on issues specific to the subject of providing gifted education. Thus, an important question asks how teachers identify a child as gifted and talented. This question is guided by the understanding that when gifted students have been identified per district standards, their talents can be cultivated in a variety of ways, such as "cooperative learning, simulations, incubation and reflection time, emotional awareness activities, physical activities, relaxation techniques, and individual projects" (Abadzi, Martelli, & Primativo, 2014, p. 27).

However, such activities should take place in traditional classroom settings, where all students can participate. Though not all students are likely to derive the same stimulation from such mainstream enrichment, successful programs will not be exclusive to those with a certain level of intellectual capability. Rather, these will create the open-ended flexibility that will allow the most gifted students to express themselves in ways that are indicative of both stimulation and growth. One may then question whether teachers have received the professional development to meet the needs of the gifted and talented. The answer to this research question determines, at least some extent, how well the teacher can balance these activities and the needs of specific students.

Researchers, Baudson & Preckel, 2013; Cross et al., 2010; Geake & Gross, 2008, highlighted the necessity to ensure that our gifted students are given access to the best possible opportunities through which to see their talents cultivated. It had long been practiced in most

U.S. public school districts that if any program was designed to cater to the unique demands of gifted students, it was an exclusive course of study (Swan, Coulombe-Quach, Huang, Godek, Becker & Zhou, 2015).   Often, this course would necessitate that students be removed from the normal classroom setting and sequestered to a class exclusively comprised of gifted students. As such, lesson plans would exist across a wide range of enrichment activities.

However, several flaws existed in this approach. For example, separating the gifted included moving them into social isolation based on their talents, with their presence in special classes carrying a social stigma and inviting the potential for resentment from students who were not entitled to an excuse from regularly scheduled curriculum (Swan et al., 2015). While this may be of secondary concern when considering the more important role that such education could play in a student's future, there are also indications that the enrichment activities do not necessarily provide gifted students with stimulation for which they are specially equipped. Or, in effect that these enrichment activities, made up of theoretical exercises and interactive projects, may not necessarily take advantage of the specific gifts of each student. In addition, it is increasingly clear that such enrichment activities could be equally beneficial to mainstream population students.

Instead, modern education experts believe that a more suitable approach is in the modification of mainstream teaching methods (Rajan et al., 2015). Rather than isolating gifted students or allowing them to fall anonymously into the general population without ever offering them the chance to flourish, it is important that educators be indoctrinated in the characteristics and needs of such pupils (Ozcan & Kotek, 2015). It is common for general education teachers to be ignorant to the specialized needs of the brightest students. This creates an unfortunately stagnant experience for such students. As Winebrenner (1999) reported,

If we define gifted as an expression of ability that exceeds the expectations for age-appropriate learners and define learning as forward progress from one's entry point into a learning curve, it becomes obvious that those students who already know what is about to be taught will not be learning as much as those students who are novices in that same content. (p. 12)

One of the most problematic institutional obstructions to proper identification of such students is a complete diagnostic dependency upon the grading system and standardized Intelligence Quotient testing. These, however, fail to encompass the wide range of permutations for what classifies a gifted student because "when educational researchers looked at highly successful creative producers, they discovered many of these movers and shakers" came from a much wider band of intellectual ability than previously thought. Objectively, "their IQs ranged between the 85th and 99th percentiles" (Cooper, 1995, p. 10). This indicates that evaluations of gifted students must move beyond these cut and dry numbers.

Educational experts have re-examined the ways in which gifted children are offered paths to growth, and it has become increasingly clear that such an accomplishment could only be precipitated by adequate endowment of funds, a re-education of instructional methods to better equip teachers with the training to help gifted students, and an educational format that fosters both integration and personal acceleration. According to Cooper (1995), in order for districts to undergo the relevant institutional changes to alter the prevailing perspectives on gifted students, it is necessary for such districts to adopt a five-point strategy. Herein, she assessed that primarily, a standard must be adopted for the classification of gifted students, determining whom they are and what they should be expected to achieve. From here, districts must determine a standard by which to identify the gifts and talents unique to each student. Only after making these foundational inroads in terms of conceptual location of such students, can educational institutions transition into the implementation of "specially designed services" to aid the identified students in achieving to their fullest potential (Cooper, 1995, p. 9). Hereafter, districts must determine what personnel will be needed to administer these services as well as "how the continuum of services is organized and operated" (Cooper, 1995, p. 9)

Across the country, the public is demanding change in the U.S. education system (Weingarten, 2014). The students are often accessed for and given resource education if they are found to need it. Moreover, another area of specialized education is the area of gifted education. Gifted and talented educational programs are throughout the system, and the screening process is designed to locate those students who are gifted. The screening process is supposed to be designed so that all gifted students can be identified, but researchers have shown that minority students are being overlooked for the programs (Baudson & Preckel, 2013; Cross et al., 2010; Geake & Gross, 2008). The screening process for the gifted and talented programs of the nation is affected by many factors including language barriers. In addition to the language barriers for students who do not speak English as their first language there have been studies that concluded the inability to read facial expressions and emotions on administrator's causes lower academic achievement for African American students. These and many other factors that are involved directly with the screening process for gifted and talented educational programs present the nation with a dilemma. The students who are gifted but of a minority background are being left behind in programs that they rightfully should have access too. The program's screening methods are such that the minority students cannot always show their abilities because of things other than ability itself.

It is important to conduct future studies on the screening processes and the impact those processes have on the minority students within the school system (Bowman-Perrott, deMarín, Mahadevan & Etchells, 2016). Studies can show the extent that the screening processes affect the outcome. African Americans have already demonstrated a lower achievement ability on standardized tests, and Hispanics have demonstrated that they test lower due to the language barriers (Bowman-Perrott et al., 2016). Each year thousands of children in the school system are receiving higher level thinking skill training and advanced educational opportunities because they are intellectually gifted. In the same way that the minority residents of the nation have demanded and received accommodations to account for their cultural and language differences, minority, gifted students in the school system deserve the same leveling tools for their educational playing field. Researchers have concluded that minority students are under-represented in the gifted programs and that it is directly related to the screening processes that are designed for White students (Card & Giuliano, 2015; Erwin & Worrell, 2012; Hollingworth & Keuseman, 2015).

Teacher and the Agentic

From a structural perspective, gifted students have an expanded vocabulary at an early age, combined with a high observational capacity (Ozcan & Kotek, 2015). Parents may be immune to these qualities because of their day-to-day interactivity with their child; however, that inertia is loosed when a teacher first enters the student's life (Ozcan & Kotek, 2015, p. 570). While the constructed environment is developing, the gifted student begins to feel alone, as new challenges appear to isolate the student from his or her convention (Ozcan & Kotek, 2015). This situation becomes compounded by a new expectation from both parent and teacher that the student is special, and therefore must meet a higher standard. This expectation creates a counter intuitive result in which the student amplifies other problems that heretofore were dormant (Ozcan & Kotek, 2015, p. 570). Webb (1994) argued that problems associated with gifted children begin as an overdose of help and criticism from parents and teachers when they begin to realize the student is gifted. This look toward perfectionism is promulgated, as the student's life becomes an asynchronous experience of unexpected emotional eruptions (Ozcan & Zabadi, 2015).

Ozcan and Kotek (2015) conducted an empirical study with aim and method requiring teachers to respond retrospectively about student reactions during the period of being found as gifted. The findings suggest the validity of compounding emotional pressure in the throes of becoming recognized. For example, the teachers reported that gifted students sense a lack of understanding of themselves by other people. They get bored easy, becoming distracted. The distraction leads to markers, such as terrible handwriting and difficulty with humor. They learn quickly, thereby reducing their interest in course management systems not readied for their intellectual abilities. The teachers suggested that society viewed gifted students as clever and that perception worked against the student during incidents of inevitable failure. In addition, families of gifted students feel their problems are different from other student families. This leads to added anxiety in the gifted students because the "giftedness is now becoming a structural problem, as well as an intellectual problem" (Webb, 1994, p. 417).

Generating puzzlement to these findings are accounts that there is little difference in achievement levels between gifted and nongifted students within the general classroom (Zeidner, Shani-Zinovich, Matthews & Roberts, 2005). Despite perceptions of gifted students' time and academic practice, teachers self-report that they spend relatively little time with top-performing students, further recounting that in a recent survey of gifted programs, throughout 2,000 school districts, most gifted students met only 1 to 4 hours per week (Card & Giuliano, 2014). Moreover, Makel and Wai (2016) surmised, "No gifted programs work" (p. 74). After review, it is reasonable to believe that educators of gifted individuals should work toward being juxtaposed to each other-but not in conflict.

Associated research in Coleman, Micko, and Cross (2015); Steenbergen-Hu and Olszewski-Kubilius (2016) shows a harmony of independent thought on critical thinking, however, it is interesting to note that not even the government has taken it upon itself to mandate a definition of gifted but rather to suggest a definition for further review (No Child Left Behind Act, 2002). This lack of government intervention points to the ensemble based illusory nature of the research, further directing it toward the horizontal positioning of the principal stakeholders whose needs are to be considered. Receiving equivalent weight, they are the parent, the student, and the teacher/school (Park et al., 2014). Therefore, there is much to consider at the intersection of postsecondary bound students and their perception of the IB DP.

Gifted as an Academic Prescription in Education

Gifted students, in the context of this study, who are characteristically postsecondary-bound become involved in programs endorsed as "pathway programs" (Park et al., 2014, p. 20). These programs are an amalgam of research development regarding gifted individuals that meet the expectations, within education, involving all principal stakeholders (i.e., students, parents, teachers, administrators, and many universities; Park et al., 2014). Pathway programs engage in assessments of students' success by focusing on themes that include peer relationships, teacher-student relationships, and the student construct of self-image after graduation (Bailey, Jaggars, & Jenkins, 2015). The obvious idea behind gateway programs is straightforward enough. College students with a defined roadmap for success are likely to make better decisions in whatever course they take toward the goal of a postsecondary degree. The IB DP is endorsed as a pathway program designed to provide enriched curricula for success at university (Callahan & Hertzberg-Davis, 2012).

Pathway programs resemble all organizations holding mission statements for success (Desmidt, 2016). In the IB DP, there is a construction of overall self-image and a construction of academic image, both leading to the pathway programs concept of success defined by its peer group (Park et al., 2014). This academic prescriptive process is thought as a rubric for "covering all of one's bases - to be prepared for all eventual scenarios" (Park et al., 2014, p. 146). If there is an arrogance associated with this internalized completeness, then it may contrast with the regular classroom as the research expands looking for additional imagination. This seems to represent a developing oxymoron associated with what people may believe about guided pathway programs for gifted students. Bailey et al. (2015) considered a challenge for comprehensive reform: "Are faculty and staff committed to allowing for a more ethereal examination of the education process?" (p. 6). In this regard, all stakeholders must be considered (i.e., teachers, students, and interested third parties) to provide insights into the IB (Siegle et al., 2016).

Beginning with teacher creativity, researchers sought to discover whether there is a relationship between aesthetic curriculum and transactional experiences of students (Fleet, 2007). Is there a worthwhile focus on the interaction between student and teacher? The encountered experiences between students and teachers are an important part of an evaluative study assessing whether the IB reaches higher sublimations of critical thought (Fleet, 2007). For example, do teachers teach what they already know or do they allow the process to underwrite what they may learn in the interactive process of IB academics? If the teacher proposes what he or she already believes as a transactional exchange with students, is there a prospect for transcendental thought?

In the four-subject teacher retrospective, conducted by Fleet (2007), the conclusions showed how the teacher interoperated his or her relationship with the gifted student. The study showed that there is a positive correlation between the aesthetics of the curriculum and the comingled experiences of students and teachers. The Fleet study had a prequel by Cross, Stewart, and Coleman (2003), wherein 15 gifted students were each interviewed for 50 minutes about their school experience. Their responses, in relation to the Husserl (1931, 2002) method of bracketing themes into thematic units, found that if the relationship between student and teacher be invariant of outside influence, student voice provided a significant student experience (Cross et al., 2003).

Socialization and Culture

Following a certain synergism of Cross et al. (2003), Fleet (2007), and Lope (2014) advanced an empirical comparative study between students who participated in IB and students who did not. The study attempted to align itself with the original intent of the IB (i.e., to produce global mindedness within its preview) and rely heavily on statistics that seem to remove the phenomenological prospect of global mindedness. Regardless, the study found certain anomalies in programs based on funding arrangements, the demographics between public and private within their jurisdictions, and the cultural demographics of the area, which indicated that there is not a significant difference between IB students and non-IB students examined in a broad demographic spectrum (Lope, 2014). This collection of findings between these researchers (Cross et al., 2003; Fleet, 2007; Lope, 2014) made a quick arch from individual experience to overall influence in a relatively short span. However, these provided showed a platform for potential research regarding the academic worth of the IB. My interpretation is that the Fleet (2007), Cross et al. (2003), and Lope (2014) studies were leveraged toward quantitative process relying on binomial responses. Could there be a significant difference if the studies were qualitative allowing student voice to come through by making extensive inquiry into the psyche of each study population?

International Baccalaureate Programs and Learner Profile

The International Baccalaureate's main objectives are to form inquiring and knowledgeable young minds. (Heydorn & Jesudason, 2013). At the same time, it aims to make the students more caring and culturally-sensitive. (Heydorn & Jesudason, 2013). To align with these goals, the programs strive to implement student-oriented and constructivist learning approaches that can support holistic development of the child. (Heydorn & Jesudason, 2013). IB learners, over the years, have attained a certain profile. They are knowledgeable, thinking, and reflective. According to scholars, IB learners are knowledgeable in that they are keen on knowing about all the concepts, ideas, and issues that have local and global importance. As they explore concepts and ideas, they earn in-depth knowledge and understanding of content from a wide range of disciplines (Bullock, 2014).

IB learners try to become practiced thinkers. (Heydorn & Jesudason, 2013). They have the initiative to think creatively and critically in approaching and solving complicated problems. In the process, they strive to make reasonable and ethical judgments and decisions. Further, IB learners are reflective (Bullock, 2014). They are thoughtful and considerate in their own learning experience. As they want to have the richest learning experience as possible, they do not rely on the efforts of others as they rely on their own. They assess their own strengths and evaluate their own weaknesses to support their learning and personal development.

Furthermore, in the International Baccalaureate programs, learning is not a passive experience wherein the students just receive and note what their teachers want them to learn. They do not passively receive facts. Instead, they embrace the process and internalize the knowledge being given to them by first absorbing and then actively exploring and reconstructing (Bullock, 2014). Ideally, the programs equip the students with the ability to gather information and process skills. They are equipped with the ability to collect, organize, identify, and then reform concepts being taught them. In applied practice, they do not accept what their teachers are telling them as is. The programs make the young people aware that the learning experience, and the associated skills of gathering and analyzing data are all personal. However, all these can be learned. Learning is not perceived as an innate talent so all students have the chance to make their learning a positive and worthwhile experience (Bullock, 2014). The anticipated personality profile is the students are expected to act with integrity and honesty. The IB students should be fair, just, and respectful. More importantly, they should ideally be responsible and accountable for their actions and the associated consequences (Bullock, 2014).

International Baccalaureate: A Gifted Program Choice

Researchers have evaluated how the components of the IB Program meet the needs of the gifted children without compromising their strengths (Park, Caine, & WImmer, 2014; Resnik, 2012). Some researchers especially focused on how the program meet the needs of children underrepresented such as immigrant students who demonstrate the aptitude of someone gifted and talented (Park, Caine, & WImmer, 2014; Resnik, 2012; Subotnik, 2011).

Park et al. (2014) claimed that enriched high school curricula such as the Advanced Placement and International Baccalaureate Diploma programs are usually mentioned and recommended as *pathway programs* for college or university-bound students. It was assumed that just by participating in these programs, universities, administrators, and even families were more likely to think highly of the students. Through a systematic review, Park et al. evaluated the experiences of the students who participated in these pathway programs themselves to see if what universities, administrators, and families perceive the students learn and acquire through these programs were the same as the actual experiences of the students. The researchers conducted a literature review of 20 materials published from 2013 to 2014 and found that the experience can be affected by peer relationships, teacher-student relationships, perceptions of success, self-image, and perceived preparation for the future experienced and fostered by these programs. The study did not consider, or align with, IB published material which avoids peer relationships and self-image regarding expectations along the IB continuum (Heydorn & Jesudason, 2013).

According to Subotnik et al. (2011), a gifted person cannot be determined or confirmed through ability or achievement. Instead, a student can exhibit outstanding performance because of their task commitment or the availability of the appropriate resources to achieve this. General and domain-specific abilities may form giftedness; however, other factors also exist. In this case, Subotnik et al. (2011) claimed that the IB could certainly serve to meet the needs of gifted children because it called for commitment to the rigorous curriculum.

Specifically, the needs of gifted or talented students are met by giving them access to college-level curriculum and enriching them through the in-depth study and the IB core. Thus, the IB offers significantly more compared to the traditional course of study. With an emphasis on the core, students are trained with independent, in-depth research. In addition, they are exposed to the Theory of Knowledge course, which is not usually part of the high school curriculum. Compared to the normal high school students, IB students undergo 15 hours of creativity, action, and service courses, apart from the six college-level courses they must take to experience an accelerated curriculum.

Various researchers have evaluated the IB for its effects on the gifted students who were given the opportunity to experience the accelerated learning curriculum (Culross & Tarver, 2011; Di Giorgio, 2010). Conley, McGaughy, Davis-Molin, Farkas, and Fukuda (2014) conducted a study published by IB that revealed that high school students given the chance to take IB courses were more likely to do well in college academically and socially because they are so well adjusted. In addition, Conley et al. (2014) claimed that the IB students who believed that they learned time management from the program were also more likely to recommend the program.

Di Giorgio (2010), in a case study, revealed that apart from the academic experience, parents chose to send their children in an IB program because they perceived it to offer a safe and challenging learning environment. Researchers added that they found common positive themes in AP and IB classes, such as better classroom atmosphere compared to the regular classes, prepared and committed teachers who treat the students with respect, classmates with similar interests and goals, and students with high self-confidence and pride, creating a special bond among them. However, researchers also found IB associated with several negative effects, such as students feeling alienated from non-IB students and IB students becoming too stressed from the amount of work they must finish compared to the non-IB students (Di Giorgio, 2010).

Culross and Tarver (2011) found mixed effects in their 10-year study on the perspectives from an initial group of IB students at the beginning of an IB program when compared to their perspectives after they completed the program. They found that during the first year of the program, students felt overwhelmed with their workload and had negative views of being in the program. However, when they looked back years later, the students claimed that these difficult experiences yielded them so many benefits that they felt satisfied with the program. Specifically, they cited the benefits of having college credits, being more prepared for college, and having deeper and wider knowledge.

Some researchers also cited that the IB program might be a great program for gifted students but not the best (Hemel, 2015; Kitsantas & Miller, 2015). Critics claimed that the program can help students be more motivated and creative, but it only focuses on one or two areas of passion where the students can certainly flourish instead of flourishing in all areas. Per Plucker and Callahan (2014), neither AB nor IB can represent the best program for the gifted learners. Ever increasing schools now adopt the curricular frameworks originally developed by the IB. By February 2016, 4335 schools have at least one IB program in place. Worldwide, this number already represents a more than 50% increase in the number of IB programs to date (IB, 2016a). A huge part of the increase is contributed by the East Asia region (IB, 2009a). According to Lee et al. (2016), the number of IB programs is increasing to meet the needs of middle and high social economic students. However, despite the continuous rise of IB programs, a dearth in literature remains that looked at the relationship between IB and student learning attributes, including critical thinking and other higher-order thinking.

Drake, Savage, Reid, Bernard, and Beres (2015) examined how Primary Years Program (PYP) teachers, coordinators, and administrators perceived and applied transdisciplinary instructional and learning approaches. Their findings showed that students who underwent the program obtained higher academic achievement and gained more life and career skills compared to peers. Hemelt (2015) also investigated the effects of the IB's primary years program on student performance, specifically focusing on students from Michigan and North Carolina. The impact is not similar between the two states, as expected. In Michigan, no significant differences were found between IB students and non-IB students. Both groups performed relatively similarly on the subjects of math, reading, and science. However, in North Carolina, the PYP negatively affected the mathematic performance of the learners. Similarly, in both Michigan and North Carolina, students exposed to PYP had better reading skills and comprehension compared to those in the low socio-economic backgrounds.

In particular, Kitsantas and Miller (2015) looked at how the PYP influenced the students' levels of self-efficacy and self-regulation, particularly in the study of mathematics. Findings revealed that the PYP helped the students become better at setting goals, monitoring, collaborating, and reflecting, which are all beneficial self-regulatory practices that can improve students' academic achievement overall. In addition, the findings indicated that with PYP, the already gifted students became even more engaged and strategic thinkers when solving mathematical problems. However, the findings showed that the IB PYP did not have the same effects on the average and low-achievers.

Lochmiller, Lucero, and Lester (2016) explored how teachers, students, and the administrators of the IB PYP programs across four Colombian schools perceived their experience. Results showed that these different stakeholders hold different perceptions of how these programs affected them, negatively or positively. In detail, administrators reported that they encountered difficulties in employing qualified teachers to lead the bilingual, transdisciplinary, and inquiry-based program effectively. Specifically, this called for the teachers to undergo more mentoring and ongoing professional development trainings. Successful implementation of the program to offer satisfactory learning experiences for the students require constant supervision and guidance of qualified teachers. Wolanin and Wade (2015) studied the effects of the Middle Years IB Program (MYP). In general, they evaluated

48

how participation in the MYP on their subsequent achievement in their academics. Data from a large, socio-economically diverse school district revealed that students, enrolled in MYP, could have higher level of college-readiness as measured by at least one college-ready score on their college preparatory exam.

In an interactive panel examining the effects of Diploma Program (DP), Ateskan, Onur, Sagun, Sands, and Corlu (2015) compared the impact of the IB DP to the effects of the Ministry of National Education Program in Turkey. In particular, the effects of the programs on graduate's university access and success were focused on. Results revealed that IB's DP was more cognitively demanding on the students compared to the Ministry's National Education Program; therefore, it prepared the students better for university. Former DP students all graduated at a higher rate as well. Ateskan et al. (2015) evaluated the effects generated by an international high school program on the university students of Turkey, studying their achievement and development levels. In addition, the goal of the researchers was to determine how the combined international and national curricula served to prepare the Turkish students for the university. The findings revealed that the primary difference between those who underwent the program and those who did not included their level of desire to experience and resolve an academic challenge.

Beckwitt, Van Kamp, and Carter (2015) examined the effects of implementing the IB in two school districts in the United States, specifically those generated by the DP. Results revealed that DP students often perceived themselves as having higher key nonacademic attributes because of their learning experience. Included in these non-academic attributes is being more culturally sensitive, having better study habits, and being more prepared for college.

Bergeron (2015) also evaluated the DP's effects specifically on the rate of enrollment in college and post-secondary outcomes. Analyzing data from students who graduated in 2008 from both public and private high schools revealed that DP could have a positive impact on college enrollment after high school. The results demonstrated that 78% of 2008 DP graduates immediately enrolled for postsecondary education. In addition, 14% enrolled after 2014. Moreover, college achievement also improved, as exhibited by the college graduation rate. The average 6-year college graduation rate for all the DP students at 83%, which equated to 27% higher than the national average of 56% graduation rate (Bergeron, 2015).

Gordon, Vander Kamp, and Halic (2015) examined trends in Title I schools in the United States that have IB program offerings. Apart from the trends, they also evaluated how the program affected Title I school students' interest and pursuance of college. Their results revealed that low-income and minority students along with their counterparts enrolled in college at a higher rate compared to the national enrollment average.

Wright (2015) examined the long-term effects of being in an IB program among those who already experienced the program. Instead of just focusing on college readiness and college achievement, Wright evaluated how IB students fared after college. The author explored IB alumni perceptions of the professional opportunities that opened for them, their career pathways, their participation in communication service projects and works, their attitudes toward lifelong learning, and their personal values after they graduated from college. Included in the examination of long-term effects was how the former IB students perceived the world and the value of diversity. Results showed that IB programs have lasting effects beyond college readiness and graduation. Results particularly revealed that the experience of an IB student could be profound and long lasting. The findings specifically showed that the IB program not only motivated them to pursue and graduate from college, but also influenced them to do well after. The students' career pathways were positively influenced by their experience; through these experiences, they could acquire an internationally minded worldview. Moreover, the former IB students also reported that because of this particular phase in their lives, they acquired positive attitudes toward lifelong learning (Wright, 2015).

Lüddecke (2015) evaluated whether one could consider the IB program as authentic. The author evaluated the program against the modern concepts associated with educational authenticity. Results indicated that the IB program could not be considered authentic just yet, even if certain aspects in the PYP curriculum derived from the philosophies of educational authenticity. MacRaild (2015) specifically evaluated the effects of the IB program on gifted students in Qatar. Results indicated that the MYP met the learning needs of the students and that the program was shaped by the neighboring Arab countries. In particular, MacRaild showed that IB has profound effects on the social values being acquired by the students through their history education. Their results revealed that IB students learned how to be more independent and critical in encountering, interpreting, and comprehending history.

Alternative Taxonomy

One study proposed a different taxonomy. Chen (2015) evaluated the roles of perceived parenting behaviors and the racial groups that the students belong to, whether they are Asian Americans or White students. Chen found that Asia American IB students have higher GPAs compared to their White IB counterparts, even though their end-of-course exam scores revealed the two groups performed relatively the same, with no significant differences in their scores to indicate one benefitted more from the program. One more significant finding included that Asian American IB students and White IB students held different perceptions of their parents' behaviors, which could affect how they performed. Specifically, the White IB students felt that their parents were more responsive and gave them a higher level of autonomy. Conversely, Asian American IB students perceived a higher level of demandingness from their parents, which for some could feel encouraging, but others found it demotivating. In addition, Fitzgerald (2015) evaluated the perception of admissions officers of the IB DP in Canadian Universities. The officers were asked to differentiate the DP from other curricula and reveal its advantages and disadvantages. Results showed the officers felt that IB, compared to other curricula, played an important role in student academic achievement.

Certain researchers revealed that teacher practices for preparing IB students into becoming globally minded citizens remain inadequate (Chatlos, 2015; Quayno, 2015). Regardless of the positive reports of IB students becoming more prepared to deal with college and their lives after graduating from a postsecondary institution with a culturally sensitive and open mind, Quaynor (2015) found otherwise. Examining how teachers of two different IB public schools prepare IB students, the results indicated that an IB program is not a guarantee that global education can be had even if a student is exposed to a diverse student body. Chatlos (2015) found the same; for example, the evidence showed that the IB program still had to improve, and one could not consider it as effective because it was highly affected by teachers' biases. The researcher designed a study to understand how teachers perceived IB learner profile traits and how these perceptions influenced how they taught the students. The author gathered in-depth data from five middle school teachers employed in an independent school located in Dallas, Texas that had an IB program in place. Results indicated that teachers seemed more inclined to utilizing certain terms repeatedly compared to different terms. The problem included that this indication revealed teachers' biases and subjectivity in the program. For the terms they seemed to favor, they carried out special and explicit strategies.

Hearon (2015) designed an in-depth study of the stress that IB students experience and evaluated how the overwhelming feelings affected their academic performance. The coping mechanisms employed by the high school students in accelerated academic curricula were also examined. Both IB and AP students experience significant amount of stress, the findings revealed. However, it was found that this did not hinder them from being satisfied with their learning experiences (Hearon, 2015). Conversely, Perna et al. (2015) claimed that access to IB programs was not equal for all, even if one was truly a gifted and advanced student. Perna et al. (2015) claimed that just like other educational opportunities, unequal access exists. They found that low-income families and racial/ethnic minority groups are not provided with the same opportunities to participate and benefit from the IB-DP in the United States.

International Baccalaureate and Critical Thinking

There are limited studies designed to evaluate the effects of IB on students' higher-order thinking as opposed to the program's effects on students' academic achievement. Aktasa and Guvenb (2015) designed one of these few studies, but in the Turkish context. They evaluated objectives, content, teaching-learning process, and evaluation process involved in the IB DP Language A1 program and compared the results against the Turkish national literature curricula. Results revealed how promising the DP is, with all the processes involved gearing the students to acquire a higher level of critical thinking skills compared to students in the national literature program. Béneker, van Dis, and Middelkoop (2015) also examined how the IB-DP influenced the world-mindedness of the students. They evaluated the effects of the program that conventional Dutch schools. Results revealed that students have higher levels of world-mindedness and have better ideas, as well as scores on their geography education, compared to students in the mainstream Dutch schools.

Cole et al. (2015) also examined the effects of IB's on the critical thinking skills of Austrian students. They started by reviewing literature on how critical thinking is effectively taught. Then, the authors evaluated if the teachers of the "Theory of Knowledge" subject in the IB DP effectively equipped the students with critical thinking skills. The course was chosen because it leadership specifically designed it to develop the students' critical thinking and learning skills. Results indicated that both secondary and high school students experienced improvements in their critical thinking skills.

In relation to determining what the effects of the IB are on students' broader and more critical thinking, Froman (2015) specifically evaluated how an IB DP human rights course effectively equipped the students with human rights knowledge and understanding. In addition, Froman evaluated if the course achieved the goals of a successful human rights education. The researcher compared the IBDP's human rights syllabus to the Article 2.2 of the United Nations' Universal Declaration on Human Rights and Training. Results showed that the IB DP human rights course needed improvement. Conversely, it allowed students to think widely and deeply about human rights because it included sufficient content on the topic. In contrast, the comparison to the U.N. declaration revealed that it lacked pedagogical practices based on human rights principles and did not motivate the development of student advocacy.

Another study that evaluated critical thinking skills associated with the IB program included Gleek's (2015) investigation. Gleek examined how students engaged in classroom simulations in an IB Global Politics course called Power, Sovereignty, and International Relations. Their learning outcomes were assessed, which led to the findings that high levels of engagement and connection to the concepts could be facilitated by the IB curriculum. Conversely, Halic, Bergeron, Kuvaeva, and Smith (2015) looked at the effects of the IB Bilingual Diploma and if it positively fostered achievement and better career pathways. Results were promising; for example, data from graduating students across 139 countries showed that BD completion was high and could lead to better career pathways. However, native language served as a moderator for these findings. Findings revealed that the chances of completing the program are higher among bilinguals or non-native English speakers compared to native English speakers.

More researchers posited that IB could improve international or global mindedness (Pitre, 2015; Poonoosamy, 2015). Pitre specifically explored how Canadian expatriate educators of overseas IB DP equipped their students with international-mindedness. Results indicated that students successfully acquire this mindedness if their teachers utilized personal history self-study. Poonoosamy studied the same, but in the context of the Indian Ocean Island Nation. Poonoosamy evaluated how two students at an IB school acquired international mindedness and found that apart from their teachers' efforts, the students' backgrounds, cultures, and local identities influenced their senses of engagement and empathy with the notion of international mindedness.

Per Wright and Lee (2014), there is increasing literature emphasizing the need for schools to equip their students with 21st century skills. Meaning, students should have both cognitive and non-cognitive skills, apart from learning about subject content and technical skills. Wright and Lee perceived the IB program as the key. The researcher explored the program's potential in helping students acquire 21st century skills in China, which is one of the fastest-growing markets for IB schools around the world. Using a multi-site case study involving five elite IB DP schools in China, Wright and Lee found that IB educational philosophy could be effective in 21st-century skills development. It does this through the provision of the three IB DP core requirements of (a) creativity, action, and service, (b) extended essay (EE), and Theory of Knowledge (TOK). However, leadership still faced some limitations and barriers in implementing this theory.

Intercultural understanding

According to Hill and Saxton (2014), in the hands of effective and reputable educators, IB presents high value to the students. Moreover, the researchers found that skills for the future have a striking match with IB outcomes, making IB students hirable and successful. DP graduates not only perform well in higher education but they also improve the reputation of the schools with these IB programs. More importantly, results showed that students who graduated from an IB program are likelier to be imbued with values of international mindedness. These values are valued by universities and desired by employers, along with cognitive attributes. However, Hill and Saxton (2014) claimed a dearth in qualitative longitudinal studies could serve as empirical evidence of these claims. Instead, most of the literature used anecdotal evidence to support their claims.

Lineham (2013) claimed that the IB organization, through its three programs (Primary Years Program, Middle Years Program, and pre-university DP), was aiming to produce students who could contribute to a more peaceful world by equipping them with intercultural understanding and respect for diversity. Lineham designed the study to measure the extent to which the program was effective in achieving these designed intentions. To do so, a growing body of research was evaluated and reviewed to determine the aims and objectives of international education.

While doing the literature review, Lineham (2013) explored the concepts found and compared these to the IB DP. The review of literature was concluded with a model that demonstrates how international education specifically affects the students within a school. The researcher then put forward a case study of an international school with an IB DP through a mixed methods approach and with an exploratory sequential design. Interviewing some IB DP students and triangulating the responses with questionnaire data completed by all DP students in the case study school, Lineham found that various ways influence how the IB DP could shape student attitudes. Findings of the study led to the conclusion that IB DP achieved its designed intent. The values of the students in question were all moving towards those highlighted and detailed in the IB mission statement. Different elements of the school curriculum and the school environment have been highlighted to serve as mediating factors, such as teachers' competency and self-efficacy levels (Lineham, 2013).

Saavedra (2014) utilized interview and survey methods to describe how IB DP specifically influenced or shaped students' "academic civic mindedness" and "model citizenship" across four public schools in California (p. n4). Results showed that the DP pedagogy provided opportunities to students to develop many of the skills necessary to carry out effective civic advocacy and that the DP equipped the students strongly with knowledge about public policy issues. In addition, the DP solidified students' sense of citizenship by inculcating in them a stronger awareness of political and social issues; at the same time, it emphasized the need for them to be engaged actively with a national or global issue. Many IB students and teachers perceive that the DP can effectively foster students' academic civic mindedness and model citizenship at a significantly greater extent compared to other curricular alternatives. In addition, the teachers felt that the strongest limitation to their prioritization of students' citizenship development included their lack of clarity on how to frame the civic implications of what they teach.

One of the main challenges is making sure that the IB curriculum can always focus on the global contexts and offer the best knowledge from different cultures and countries instead of one source. (Heydorn & Jesudason, 2013). At the same time, however, this dares highlight why the IB's curriculum with its current focus on global contexts and aspiration can lead to critical thinking. According to Castro, Lundgren, and Woodin (2015), one important reason why students are attracted to the international baccalaureate programs is because they believe these programs can equip them with the international mindedness, which is perceived as the major factor in their career and life plans. The prevalent assumption is that IB programs offer the students the chance to experience more meaningful learning, access to important linguistic tools, and the chance to acquire intercultural understandings so that they can think critically when pursuing global engagements and goals (Castro et al., 2015).

In addition, critical thinking is more likely to be developed through an IB education because students are given the opportunity to study through a broad and yet balanced conceptual as well as connected curriculum (Menendez, 2015). Compared to other curriculum, students do not rigidly study specific content. Students have access to a wide range of content that covers different academic subjects. As students transcends from PYP, to MYP, DP and IBCC, their ability to engage subject-specific knowledge and carry out certain skills becomes more sophisticated and effective. In addition, conceptual thinking is encouraged, which leads students to become better critical thinkers. Learning is focused on acquiring knowledge about and organizational ideas spanning different subject areas. Course aims and requirements in majority of IB programs offer the ability to learn about the world (Menendez, 2015).

Summary

In the main, the completed literature review investigated among development orgasmic versions of Gestalt and Field theories, as they may relate to the IB model. In addition, the current state of critical thinking among students was reviewed. The literature established that the notion of critical thinking has evolved as new schools of thought led to new insights that changed out of date lines of reasoning. As such, the concept of logical or critical thinking is expected to change again in the future as new ideas are presented. Therefore, critical thinking has and will continue to evolve. More than ever, critical thinking skills are 21st century skills that schools' leadership and educators must provide to their graduates. Well-educated students need effective critical thinking skills to make well-informed judgments and explain their reasoning. Critical thinking also gives students the chance to arrive at solutions to complicated problems. Therefore, it is a crucial goal for individual instructors to provide explicit instructions (and training) regarding critical thinking strategies and skills to all, including gifted and talented students.

The review of literature revealed that gifted students are often presumably and characteristically postsecondary-bound, which is why they are encouraged to undergo programs endorsed as "pathway programs" (Park et al., 2014, p. 20). These programs are developed to meet the expectations, within education, involving all principal stakeholders (e.g., the students, parents, teachers, administrators, and many universities; Park et al., 2014). Pathway programs are assessed using how students developed better peer relationships, teacher-student relationships, as well as positive student constructs of self-image after graduation (Bailey et al., 2015). Among these programs is the IB DP, which is designed to provide enriched curricula for success at university (Callahan & Hertzberg-Davis, 2012).

Several studies have shown that indeed, the IB programs have been helpful for the gifted students. Researchers have revealed that the IB program encourage the students to entertain postsecondary education and enroll in college (Gordon et al., 2015; Wright, 2015). In addition, IB effects on the students are long lasting. The experience of an IB student can be very profound, which not only motivated students to pursue and graduate from college, but also influence them to do well in college and in their respective careers. Researchers have also found that IB can help students acquire an internationally minded worldview and have positive attitudes toward lifelong learning (Wright, 2015). There are limited studies that evaluated effects of IB on students' higher-order thinking as opposed to the program's effects on students' academic achievement but the few that did, revealed how promising the DP is, with all the processes involved gearing the students to acquire a higher level of critical thinking skills compared to students in the national literature program. However, more research is needed.

Chapter 3: Research Method

The development of this phenomenological research study rises from the premise that (Graduated) high school students have distinctive perspectives in their education experience, specifically in the International Baccalaureate Program (IB) at a Western Washington regional high school. The research allowed former students interpretation in authentic free-flowing conversation to build an understanding of their defined experience in IB education to establish if their interpretation was congruent with the published goals of IB education, and to learn from these student and faculty voices where best practices might be applied to the IB. This chapter discussion finds its ethos in the interpretation of the research question:

Research Question 1. What are IB students lived experiences regarding the transactional and transcendental /transpersonal synthesizing of their critical skills leading to higher order thinking during, and after graduating from, the IB Diploma Program?

The purpose of this phenomenological research study was to understand the nuances of transcendental education and why higher order thinking was not being achieved within the IB. Qualitative research methods that focus on phenomenology were the best way to consider the IB derivation of knowledge because qualitative reports give rich descriptions of interrelated environments, which can be accompanied by interpretations of influences (Moustakas, 1995). Grand collections of expressions work well when seen through the lens of experience based methodology.

The research sample was used to explore the phenomenological experiences of five high school IB graduates who were exposed to IB prescriptive pedagogy. Teaching styles were discussed by the students to explore their phenomenological experiences. Using assessment developed by Stake and Munson (2008), the researcher sought to provide appraisal of the student and faculty understandings of IB education from the qualitative perspective as first-hand, true-to-life, and systematic interpretations. The aggraded experience of student and faculty voices may serve to deepen administrator and faculty introspection, potentially leading to curative measures.

Research Methods

This study used phenomenology, i.e., phenomenological reduction, to investigate the perceptions of students regarding their lived experience in the IB DP classroom environment, and how that experience carried forward after the fact. Further, to establish if the qualitative experience transcends the transactional nature of commonplace learning. Phenomenology uses reflective meditation rooted in *contemplative honesty* first established by the mid and late-20th Century by existential philosophers Edmund Husserl 1859-1938, Martin Heidegger 1889-1976, and Maurice Merleau-Ponte 1908-1961 (Moustakas, 1995). Among these, it was Husserl who established phenomenological reduction as a research method for what has become known as "seeing things as they are" (Huntington, 2016; McIntyre & Graziano 2016; Riener, 2015). *Reduction* is as it implies developing a role in the qualitative information's diagnostic process. The appropriateness of phenomenological reduction to this studies purpose lies in the Epoche of coming to a knowing awareness. *Knowing*, in this context, is seeing things free of judgments and preconceptions (Moustakas, 1995). This quality of experience became the focus of the inquiry. Metaphorically, each angle of personal reflection brings a refined perspective. These refinements come to be reductions leading to intent i.e., "to the things themselves" (Moustakas, 1995, p.91). The associated multi-layered perceptions become transcendental because they uncover the individuality from which everything presents meaning (Moustakas, 1995). Thus, to understand the character of realism within this studies research sample, there had to be an investigation of the perceptive process governing lived experience specific to the IB DP (Tong, 2016).

Design Steps

To look again and again. This description is deceiving. It suggests ease of process; however, reductions are reflective. For this study, they required stratifications of process i.e., layering content to identify descriptions of behavior within the IB DP culture. Looking again and again for motives, values, beliefs, and attitudes in speech. These became stylistic idiosyncrasies unique to each research subject. There is a great deal of emotional depth associated with this reduction process. The co-researchers – interviewer and interviewee – returned again and again for clarification and validation. Researchers interested in attempts at duplication of the reduction process must be willing to spend disproportionate amounts of time – leading to emotional depth – with a select group of informed participants. The time spent provides thematic overlays, based on repetitive examination of underlying linguistic characteristics, leading to important and interesting insights for all stakeholders.

Structural Codes

In qualitative inquiry codes are usually words or short phrases that symbolize meaning – all leading to a summative conclusion (Saldana, 2013). These inquiries are considered as *cycles* and they are as they imply – a returning again and again through intuitive exercise (Saldana, 2013). Each coding cycle occupies as much or as little of the subject content as seems appropriate. This layering of thought, comingled with various amounts of content, is what leads to the refinement necessary for an approach to replication later. Saldana (2013) describes a code as a "research-generated construct" capturing meaning associated with datum (p.4). The later purpose of this type of research-generated construct is to establish theory building using the evolving essence of the content. It is Important for the researcher and co-researchers to reflect on all possible influences in qualitative investigations. For example, contextual characteristics should be viewed in perspective due to culture, gender, and geopolitical influence should that situation apply. It is these context rich examinations that support the developing structural codes capable of sustaining a peer review (Finfgeld-Connett & Johnson, 2013). The understandable adverse outcomes being that shallow saturation in these interrelated findings become a threat to the trustworthiness of the study (Finfgeld-Connett & Johnson, 2013).

The strong objection to narrative speech coding is that it does not work. "It is impossible in practice" (Packer, 2011, p. 80). The assumption being, speech analysis using a combination of linguistics and intuition cannot be replicated later. Researchers preparing qualitative research experiences have never been unconscious of the antagonism from members of the hard sciences concerning interpretative/subjective scholarship. The admonishment from the hard science side being that search of truth has become so influenced by political correctness that the thrust of science is redefining empirical evidence so that all truth is no more than an interpretation (Drake, 2002). For skeptics, it is difficult to make dogma from multiple interpretations bereft of binary precision. Conversely, MIT linguist Noam Chomsky, and Harvard Professor Steven Pinker built impressive academic careers demonstrating that space and time are embedded with words leading to causality (Chomsky & Barsamian, 2015; Pinker, 2007). The human model of reality is codified in speech, a *soft science* (Pinker, 2002).

I am a spectator in this world of contemporary soft and hard science politics. The place where some suggest soft science is the state of pretense where prizes are given for the most preposterous conclusion (Drake, 2002). To this there is a contrarian example from hard science itself as Einstein's philosophy is politely shelved in Agassi (2015).

Einstein considered fallibilist methodology obvious and metaphysics the challenging heuristic of physics. This philosophy is a minority view in academic philosophy. Most commentators on Einstein reject it and either refuse to ascribe it to him or declare it an impediment to his researches, his own opinion to the contrary notwithstanding.

Therefore, is replication possible in qualitative research? In Agassi (2015), as well as in Crease & Goldhaber, (2014), and the EPR Paper co-authored by Einstein, Podolsk, and Rosen in 1935 the scientists agreed:

> Any serious consideration of a physical theory must take into account the distinction between the objective reality, which is independent of any theory, and the physical concepts with which the theory operates. These concepts are intended to correspond with the objective reality, and by means of these concepts we picture this reality ourselves. (p. 199)

The EPR paper has become one of the most famous scientific papers of all time as it evokes the reality of the quantum (Crease & Goldhaber 2014). Therefore, traditional binary replication in the *clockwork* Newtonian world must be open to scrutiny in the face of modern quantum mechanics/metaphysics (Rosenblum & Kutter, 2011). There is no paradox in Newtonian action/reaction. People's movements are trackable through binary interpretation, therefore, Newton's Laws (Rosenblum & Kutter, 2011). Motives however, are shifty not necessarily making sense. Nevertheless, there is a pragmatic day-to-day acceptance of motive when dealing with people (Rosenblum & Kutter, 2011). This is the epiphany of uncertainty that struck Heisenberg, Bohr, and Born as Einstein abandoned his attachment to classical determination (Crease & Goldhaber, 2014, p. 190). What they came to agree collectively, including Einstein, and what I believe today, is that research – in this case, qualitative research `-

is a humanist's interpretation of thought in a segment of space and time worthy of additional study (Din, 2016).

Population

The participants were selected out of a general population of students in the (FWPS) Federal Way Public Schools IB DP in the Pacific Northwest, USA. The school district encompassing this population is responsible for 22,511 students and families, and 2,500 staff members in 39 schools (FWPS, p. 2611). The population demographic is: 22,511 students

67.8% Ethnicity other than white

59.2% Free & Reduced

16.5% Transitional/bilingual

13.5% Special Ed (FWPS, p. 2612)

The specific population for this study were students in the IB DP graduated from Thomas Jefferson High School within the FWPS district. Members of the sample were distinguished from the general population as being graduated from the IB DP. The population is appropriate to respond to the study problem and purpose because since 1995, the FWPS district has modified its academic focus toward creating a post-secondary culture in their secondary schools. All students in the FWPS take advanced program tests at district expense. Only Thomas Jefferson High School in the FWPS system offers the IB DP to FWPS students (FWPS, p. 202). The channeling of IB DP students to Thomas Jefferson High School provides a decidedly select cohort from the overall FWSD student population.

Sample

The sample consisted of student participants each meeting a criterion (see below) to help insure validity through a purposeful selection (Bishop & Yardley, 2007; Creswell, 2014; Denzin

& Lincoln, 2011). The number of participants allowed for saturation in the context of existing phenomenological research methods (Mason, 2010). The most commonly cited subject examples from phenomenology are: Creswell (1998, p.64) five to 25; Morse (1994, p.225) at least six (Mason, 2010). From the literature, deep discussions with five participants met accepted phenomenology sampling traditions and developed into perspective saturation with no nascent patterns (O'Reilly, Michelle, & Parker, Nicola, 2012). A significant departure form Creswell (1998, p.64) five to 25; Morse (1994, p.225) at least six (Mason, 2010), is that 'one' interview can be examined as several occurrences. Therefore, from this perspective, a set of cultural understandings can have a phenomenology develop around 'one' subject (Kohn & Sydnor 2006).

There remain discursive approaches to saturation in phenomenology (Creswell, 2014). Conversely, it endures as thought-provoking that traditional binary instrumented researchers, whose protagonists suggest the marginalized worth of phenomenological enquiry validity (Kauffman, 2014), remain reasonably satisfied when *one elementary particle* strikes a photographic paper (anywhere) to leave an imprint in an unexplainable random fashion (Mabrok, Dong, Petersen & Chen, 2014; Rosenblum & Kuttner, 2011).

From specific criterion, random selections were not associated with this study. The student samples from the population were selected and vetted in advance for academic achievement. The interview environments were at the Seattle Public Library (SAP). All invitations were one-on-one actualities between subject and researcher. The interviews were open ended, running for as long as necessary, with no specific limitations. The interviews were electronically transcribed, reviewed for accuracy, and prescribed by descriptive coding.

Materials/Instrumentation

In the Methods and Design section of this chapter I reintroduce the mid and late-20th Century existential philosophers Edmund Husserl (1859-1938), Martin Heidegger (1889-1976), and Maurice Merleau-Ponte (1908-1961). These philosophers, in their work, represent the meaning of *lived experience* as a distillation of the human condition (Bloomberg & Volpe, 2012). This condition presents itself as *phenomena*, the selected research method for this study (Moustakas, 1994).

The instrument used to support analytic memos through multiple cycles of interpretation was opened-ended conversational interviews (Silverman, 2013). To meet the conditions of this study, the interviewer followed the Moustakas (1994) suggestion that the interview process be informal, and face-to-face (p. 103-119). There was interview guide – formed as a litany of 22 structured questions. The questions were implicit to the IB DP, and formed an aggregated platform for bracketing (Epoche) i.e., the researcher interjecting his or her understandings of the individual experiences demonstrated by the research subjects (Bloomberg & Volpe, 2012, p.32). The research questions were not identified to the students in advance of the interviews.

Study Procedures

Agreement between the sole researcher and the student subjects was ratified. Upon this ratification approval from the Institutional Review Board (IRB) of NCU was required. Proprietary transcription equipment software was used by the researcher to record verbatim data from the participants. All recordings were reviewed for clarification with changes to specifically identified datum as necessary. In this study, the final assembler of information worked through examination of *subject voice* using analytic memos. Therefore, it is appropriate to remind the reader, as I did previously in Research Methods and Design(s) that the final data can be devious, not necessarily following the binary notations of Newtonian logic. Nevertheless, there is a practical day-to-day acceptance of motive when dealing with people (Rosenblum & Kutter, 2011).

Data Collection

The collection and analysis proceeded along a continuum of voice/text interpretation strategies. In descending order, developing conceptual approaches through review, and re-examination for outcomes to be condensed. The text was once again re-visited for revision. Finally, to produce reports of findings and terminal analysis (Bloomberg & Volpe, 2012, p. 140). This was a comprehensive overview that fundamentally related the material to the research questions. The relevant outcomes were prescribed being flexible and emergent. The transcript was again, re-visited for reconsideration. The descriptors are suggestive portrayals of the actualities. From here the text was truncated to more manageable formats to produce reports of findings. Then the process moved toward analytic memos of context summary providing conclusions and recommendations. The pervasive themes are identified as *findings* in Chapter Four. Finally, in Chapter Five, to produce terminal analysis, the final stage brings the story as objectively as possible - seeing the things themselves – as they are in the tradition of transcendental phenomenology (Moustakas, 1994).

This is the intuitive grasp of reality that struck participants' in the Copenhagen interpretation in 1925-1927 as Einstein began to abandon his attachment to ontological principals in classical determination (Crease & Goldhaber, 2014). What researchers came to agree collectively, as classical scientists', and participants in the Copenhagen interpretation, is that research is a humanist's interpretation of thought in a segment of space and time worthy of additional study (Din, 2016). According to the Copenhagen interpretation, the world exists in two very different domains; "all we can ultimately know of the world prior to observation is a set of probabilities" (Crease & Goldhaber, 2014, p. 190). And, in one inescapable and intractable domain, that interpretation may be driven by motive.

Data Analysis

Data analysis was conducted by following Moustakas' (1994) modified van Kaam method. The method consists of sevens steps and were all strictly followed in the study. The following steps are then presented below:

First step: Listing and preliminary grouping. The first step of the modified van Kaam method was the practice of "listing and preliminary grouping" of the experiences from the interviews of the five IB graduates. The practice of noting and citing the noteworthy and significant patterns of experiences was also known as the "horizonalization" process of the analysis (Moustakas, 1994, p. 120). The first stage also incorporated the practice of removing all bias and preconceptions on the subject being investigated on.

Second step: Reduction and elimination. The second step of the van Kaam method was the "Reduction and Elimination" process (p. 121). Moustakas (year) identified two questions to determine the invariant constituents or the other important perceptions and experiences of the interviewed participants:

(1) Does it contain a moment of the experience that is a necessary and sufficient constituent for understanding?; and

(2) Is it possible to abstract and label it? If so, it is a horizon of the experience. Expressions not meeting the above requirements are eliminated. Overlapping, repetitive, and vague expressions are also eliminated or presented in more descriptive terms. The horizons that remain are the invariant constituents of the experience. (p. 121)

70

From the two questions asked by Moustakas (year), the five transcripts of the of IB

program graduates were cautiously reviewed. The queries became the foundation to determine

which parts and aspects of the interviews were to be incorporated in the next five steps of the

phenomenological study. Meanwhile, the lived experiences gathered were all based on the main

research question of the study as well as the formed thematic labels or categories from the

experiences shared during the interviews.

Third step: Clustering and thematizing of the invariant constituents. The third step

of the phenomenological analysis was completed by assembling and clustering the formed

invariant constituents from the second step. Moustakas (1994) explicated that the "clustered and

labelled constituents" should then be identified as the "core themes" of the analysis (p. 121).

With the help of the computer software, MAXQDA, and NVivo11 by QSR, both the invariant

constituents and core themes were systematically coded and the order of significance was

charted. The section below encompasses the findings from the third stage of the

phenomenological analysis addressing the experiences of the IB graduates and how the

transactional and transcendental /transpersonal synthesizing of their critical skills led to higher

order thinking during, and after graduating from, the IB Diploma Program.

Fourth step: Final identification of the invariant constituents and themes. The fourth

step of the phenomenological analysis was the authentication and justification of the formed

major and minor themes discussed in the third step. This course of the analysis was performed to

validate the findings; and corroborate the findings with the actual responses of the participants

found in the interview transcripts. Three other questions were suggested by Moustakas (year):

(1) Are they expressed explicitly in the complete transcription?;

(2) Are they compatible if not explicitly expressed?; and

(3) If they are not explicit or compatible, they are not relevant to the participant's experience and should be deleted. (p. 121)

Fifth step: Individual textural descriptions. The fifth step of the analysis that followed was the formation of the individual textural descriptions. In this stage of the analysis, the checked and certified major and minor themes were then used to generate the individual textural structural descriptions of the five participants. Again, verbatim responses by the participants were incorporated to support and explain the lived experiences discovered on the IB program.

Sixth step: Individual structural description. The sixth step was the constructing of the individual structural descriptions. This again employed the experiences of the five participants from the "Individual Textural Description and Imaginative Variation" step of the process (Moustakas, 1994, p. 121).

Seventh step: Textural-structural description. The final stage of the modified method by Moustakas was the integration of both the minor and major themes of the study. In this combination of experiences, the "meanings and essences" shared on the IB program were highlighted further (p. 121). The last step should then involve the shared responses of the participants on the six lived experiences discovered all connected on the transactional and transcendental /transpersonal synthesizing of their critical skills leading to higher order thinking during, and after graduating from, the IB Diploma Program.

Assumptions

In this study, it was assumed that participants believe participation in the IB DP was an important indicator of academic promise. They believed that IB DP students have an academic as well as a tactical advantage in the college admissions process. They believed that the IB DP is a prescribed collaboration between high school and college faculty regarding the IB DP. To this end the student subjects self-assessed as being gifted, and believed that they meet the general definition of gifted from the National Association of Gifted Children (NAGC: 2010). Gifted individuals are those who demonstrate outstanding levels of aptitude or competence in one or more domains. Domains include any structured area of activity with its own symbol system and/or set of sensorimotor skills (para. 1). The matrix establishing the parameters for the selection assumptions are: Participating Students were graduated from the IB DP at Thomas Jefferson High School. They had an earned post-secondary degree. They were in the workplace or a combination of workplace and graduate school. By meeting these parametric assumptions an adequate response rate and participant honesty was assumed thereby providing the researcher with discernable reactions.

Limitations

The sample size was not a limiting consideration in this case as the sample met the typical phenomenology study size considered satisfactory for thematic development leading to saturation (Creswell, 2014; Moustakas, 1994; Silverman, 2013). To maintain phenomenology design integrity, the studied underpinnings of qualitative research were brought to bear through the lived experiences of the subjects. There has been a great deal of discussion in this study regarding the relative worth of subjective interpretation in science. One must remain in focus that checking the accuracy and validity of a persons lived experience though that person's voice is different than an explanatory sequence of binary precision (Silverman, 2013). The triangulation one expects from Grounded Theory, Ethnography or Case Studies is replaced with stratified revisiting of the subject in a phenomenological reduction to begin to see the conversation essence free of all external influences. A pure as possible demonstration of Epoche – seeing things as they are (Moustakas, 1994).

Delimitations

The delimitations narrowing this study rest in the studies assumptions. The subjects coalescing around tight experience parameters leading to high academic and ethical performance. The expectation being that by enforcing such a selective rubric the ability to go deep in the conversation was greatly enhanced, and thereby coalesce into the results. The study's assumptions for students were that they must have been graduated from the IB DP at Thomas Jefferson High School. They had an earned post-secondary degree, and they were in the workplace or a combination of workplace and graduate school.

Ethical Assurances

In accord with the Code of Federal Regulations TITLE 45 PUBLIC WELFARE DEPARTMENT OF HEALTH AND HUMAN SERVICES - PART 46 - PROTECTION OF HUMAN SUBJECTS Revised January 15, 2009 Effective July 14, 2009. This study's subjects met the definition of participants considered to be at minimal risk and therefore would not cause physical or emotional harm to the study subjects as described in Materials and Instruments in this research material.

Permissions were granted through informed consent in advance, and IRB approval was sought prior to any data collected. There were clear understandings between the sole researcher, and the population subjects. Subjects who choose to participate in this research were asked to respond to far-reaching questions. Although the potential risks associated with this study were minimal; subjects could have experience some stress if a question caused a recall of a negative experience.

All participants maintained the right to withdraw from the study at any time and without recourse of any kind from any source. The agreement used nomenclature easily understood by a common man in the Blackstone Common Law orthodoxy "the undistinguished commoner lacking class or rank distinction or special attributes" (Kadens, 2009).

All interviews were conducted in an environment familiar to the research subsects. The information housed this study will remain as the preview of the sole researcher, the academic staff and assigns thereto at NCU, and subjects themselves for purposes of clarification. The material will be locked-out to all other interested third parties. Should the material be published, it will be under the guidelines of the NCU IRB and the United States Library of Congress. Should there be learning associated with this study, that learning remains the property of the researcher and NCU as that bilateral contract may appear.

Summary

Qualitative inquirers understand common features of human science research (Moustakas, 1994). In that tradition, this study utilized methodologies associated with the exploration human experience as opposed to human reaction (Silverman, 2013). This study has as its focus the wholeness of the subjects' experiences i.e., human voice within the context of the IB DP and life going forward (Bloomberg & Volpe, 2012). This study's sample became involved in deep discussions meeting accepted phenomenology sampling traditions and developed into a research subject perspective saturation with no nascent patterns (O'Reilly, Michelle, & Parker, Nicola, 2012). This because small samples better associate with deep discussions, and are easier to manage than large samples that may not allocate the necessary time to meet the validation demands of emotional depth present in a well-constructed phenomenology (Creswell, 2014. p. 197). Further, this study used a defined set of parameters in the subject selection process eliminating forms a sampling errs due to a subject distribution that installs outliers not suited to the acumen necessary for the question at hand (Saldana, 2013). Finally, this study reflects the interest, involvement, and personal commitment of the researcher. The meanings and essences from the first-person accounts finding their way out of this research will add to a knowledge base within the social science community that will increase the efficiencies visited upon students in the IB DP.

Chapter 4: Findings

The purpose of this qualitative phenomenological research study was to understand the lived experience of IB students and why higher order thinking may not be achieved within the IB. One main research question guided the study: What are IB students' lived experiences regarding the transactional and transcendental /transpersonal synthesizing of their critical skills leading to higher order thinking during, and after graduating from, the IB Diploma Program? To better address the main research question, six thematic labels were formed based on the interviews, these were the: (1) early education experiences; (2) graduation experiences; (3) overall IB program experiences; (4) education philosophy experiences from the IB program; (5) IB program faculty experiences; (6) IB socialization experiences. Moustakas' (1994) modified van Kaam's method was utilized to analyze the interviews with the participants. The seven-step analysis was employed to carefully extract the meanings from the experiences shared by the participants. NVivo11 software by QSR was also used to aid in the systematic coding of the established themes. This chapter should also contain the following: demographics, trustworthiness of data, findings with the formed themes and verbatim responses of the participants, evaluation of findings, and a brief summary of the chapter.

Demographics

Participants of the study were five-high school IB graduates who were exposed to IB prescriptive pedagogy. Three participants were males and two were females. All participants were 27 years old during the time of the interview. All participants were from the University of Washington. Table 1 contains the breakdown of participant demographics. The demographics of the participants are presented to gain a better understanding of their background in light of their shared perceptions and experiences.

Table 1

Breakdown of the Participant Demographics

	Gender	Age	University
Participant 1	Male	27	University of Washington
Participant 2	Female	27	University of Washington
Participant 3	Male	27	University of Washington
Participant 4	Female	27	University of Washington
Participant 5	Male	27	University of Washington

Trustworthiness of Data

To ensure the trustworthiness of the study's data, four measures or indicators were guaranteed as suggested by Lincoln and Guba (1985). The first measure was the "credibility" of the results. Credibility was achieved as the researcher gathered, analyzed, and reported the perceptions of the participants or the IB students as they reported them during the interviews. In addition, credibility was substantiated as I performed a member-check and asked all participants to check and review the collected data; during the member-checking, participants were given the opportunity to review their responses and add or correct any information as needed. Another measure was the "transferability" of the study. I included the participants' background through their demographics, a detailed step-by-step procedure of the modified van Kaam analysis in Chapter 3, and the process followed in establishing the themes of the study in order to provide a thorough understanding of the research. Through these practices, the results may then be generalized or employed in other study context or research settings in the future. The third measure or indicator was the dependability of the study wherein all coding data and other raw files are made available as evidences that will address the ever-changing environment of the subject and research context. Finally, confirmability was also achieved as all documents for member-checking were certified; and a data-audit was generated to record all steps and procedures taken and that data collection and analysis processes were conducted without any bias.

Findings

The main research question that guided the study was: What are IB students' lived experiences regarding the transactional and transcendental /transpersonal synthesizing of their critical skills leading to higher order thinking during, and after graduating from, the IB Diploma Program? To address the main research question, six thematic labels or categories were generated to gain a complete understanding of the context of the research question. These are in terms of the participants': early education experience; graduation experience; overall IB program experience; education philosophy experience from the IB program; IB faculty experience; and IB socialization experience. In this section, the results or themes discovered from the modified van Kaam analysis are presented with the verbatim responses of the participants.

Thematic label 1: Early education experiences. The first thematic label pertained to the early education experiences of the participants in the context of addressing the IB students lived experiences regarding the transactional and transcendental /transpersonal synthesizing of their critical skills leading to higher order thinking during, and after graduating from, the IB Diploma Program. From the analysis, three themes were discovered. The majority of the participants shared that even during their early education, they have always strived for academic excellence. Other experiences shared were pushing for the development of the mind; and settling more contentedly with extra-curricular activities. Table 2 contains the breakdown of the themes on the early education experiences.

Table 2

Breakdown of the Themes on Early Education Experiences

Themes	Number of Participants	Percentage of Participants
Striving for academic excellence	4	80%
Pushing for the development of the mind	1	20%
Settling more contentedly with extra-curricular activities	1	20%

Major Theme 1: Striving for academic excellence. The first major theme of the study was the experience of striving for academic excellence. Under this theme, four participants (80%) indicated that they have always aimed for excellence in academic and education even during their early years. Participant 1 stated that his early education was already focused on having academic accomplishments. He shared that his early education was targeted on building his academic background to have a clear and strong educational qualifications as well as to achieve academic excellence:

Well, my early education was very focused on pushing the academic limits.

Middle school was spent going to the Federal Way Public Academy, which was a public charter school, essentially, done for the Federal Way area, which was a purely academic institution.

All right, I know exactly which classes to take. I know which degree I want. I know what the path is. I took lots of fun classes as well, but it was pretty much very strictly on this history approach.

Participant 3 believed that he was always focused on his academics even in his early education; and his transition from one school to another. Participant 3 added that he also grew up in an environment where education was always the main priority. His focus was on his academics as there were different teachers who instilled him on the significance of the education; in addition, he transitioned from one school to another but the focus remained on achieving academic accomplishments:

It was definitely more focused on academics. It was a transition from one classroom, one teacher to 6 teachers or so. It was interesting to get used to all the different teachers. There was also an interesting mix of students there because I remember it wasn't ... As a public school, anyone could go there, so it wasn't ... Since it was a lottery, there was no real application. There was no anything you had to pass. It was just if you said, or your parents said you wanted to go, you had the option to go.

Participant 4 expressed that she has always been determined to work and progress successfully to the IB program. Participant 4 believed that focusing on school should lead to the successful transition to the IB program:

Like I said, I was really focused on school, particularly in high school, so it seemed like a natural progression from the academy to the IB program. I really hadn't done public school before, so having a smaller group of classes and everything seemed a lot less intimidating, to be honest. Like I said, it just seemed like a natural progression from the academy.

Finally, Participant 5 shared that his family's background plays a big role in honing and developing his educational background. Since both his parents failed to graduate from college, they have always been determined in getting him into college and admitting him to the best institution. Participant 5 then believed that his parents had already laid the path for him to strive for academic excellence; as well as his successful career in the future:

I'm an only child. Neither of my parents graduated from college. I think it affected my dad the most. He worked for the government and could never did get above a GS-9 in federal grade because he lacked a college degree. So, I ended up with sort of a trickle-down situation in school. My parents were going to get me into and through college one way or the other and the international baccalaureate diploma program seems like a good option as far as they were concerned at the time.

Minor Theme 1: Pushing for the development of the mind. The first minor theme that followed or the other significant experience was the practice of pushing for the development of the mind. The experience was indicated by just one participant and may need further research to validate its credibility. Participant 1 stated that his early education was targeted on encouraging the development of the mind given that he was part of the kids who showed great potential: "I really felt that my early education was all purely... Kind of just encouraged the development of the mind, especially amongst kids who showed potential."

Minor Theme 2: Settling more contentedly with extra-curricular activities. The second minor theme of the thematic label was the choice of settling more contentedly with their extra-curricular activities. The minor theme was reported by just one participant and should need further research to validate its credibility. Participant 2 admitted that she was not as focused and motivated on her academics during his younger years. She believed that she was more enthusiastic with her extra-curricular activities, particularly, ballet as compared to her academics. She shared that ballet gave her the enthusiasm that she needed; and was even more vital than graduating in high school:

What most people don't like about high school is probably what I didn't like about middle school. The friends I didn't care for, I don't keep up with. But the schooling itself was good.

The Academy, that was homespun, there was a lot of love there, a lot of parent involvement so that was nice. But it wasn't the formal high school graduation or college graduation. In high school, it was just a lot of, pardon the pun, but pump and circumstance. I just ... I didn't need, I knew what I studied and I knew what I got. Comparatively, and this might be a little outside your scope, but I was a member of the British Dancing Academy for 15 years, a ballet school. That, graduating from there, was much more significant to me than graduating from high school.

I just had more ties there, just being there so long kind of my entire childhood and learning everything I did. That was just something I'd always looked forward to was having that senior show and graduating.

Thematic label 2: Graduation experiences. The second thematic label pertained to the graduation experiences of the participants. From the analysis, three themes were discovered. The majority of the participants shared how they were excited and looked forward to finally attending the graduating ceremony. Meanwhile, other participants stated that they focused more on transitioning into the actual IB program than the ceremony; and felt indifferent as they were isolated from the non-IB students. Table 3 contains the breakdown of the themes on the graduation experiences of the participants.

Table 3

Breakdown of the Themes on Graduation Experiences

Themes	Number of Participants	Percentage of Participants
Looking forward to finally graduating	3	60%
Focusing more on transitioning into the actual IB program	2	40%
Feeling indifferent and isolated from the non-IB students	1	20%

Major theme 2: Looking forward to finally graduating. The second major theme of the study was the experience of looking forward to finally graduating. Three participants (60%) stated that just like the normal students, they felt enthusiastic and anticipated their graduation. Participant 2 stated that along with her senior ballet show, she also looked forward to finally graduating: "I just had more ties there, just being there so long kind of my entire childhood and learning everything I did. That was just something I'd always looked forward to was having that senior show and graduating." Participant 4 anticipated their graduation because of the different talks and orientations aimed at preparing the students for college. From these talks, she found that the school was trying to prepare and equip them with the proper knowledge and skills for college:

I mean, there was a lot of talk about preparing us for college, and I think that was mainly my takeaway from the whole thing is that they were really trying to prep us for higher learning and being prepared for everything that was to come.

Lastly, Participant 5 believed that the experience was "good" but not as "special" as it should have been. He then described the graduation feeling and experience as "good"; however,

84

he added that it was not as special as they graduated with the general population of the school. In addition, a private ceremony was also held for the IB students before the actual graduation:

I felt good but not special. The IB at Thomas Jefferson was a class within a class. There was a group of us that studied together and went to class together for IB related subjects. Otherwise we were in the general population, and we graduated with the general population. There was a private ceremony for us before graduation- earlier in the week. That was special but was isolated so there was no demonstration of us being better than the others

Minor theme 1: Focusing more on transitioning into the actual IB program. The first minor theme that followed was the experience of focusing more on their transition into the actual IB Program in College than the graduation. The experience was shared by two participants or 40% of the sample population. Participant 1 believed that the graduation was not as important as the acceptance and transition to the IB program was more vital for him. He shared that graduation was not significant to him. This is because being part of the IB program was what mattered to him the most. He added that the graduation was a sign of moving from one institution to another:

Well, to me, it was actually not that important. Being in the International Baccalaureate program, that was what was important. That was ... Getting that degree was the rigor that you're going towards. The entire focus was less on oh, I'm going to be out of high school. It's more, I need to do well on this exam or else I'm A) not going to get the degree and B) not going to get college credit for it.

For the actual graduation experience, it was exciting in a sense, but I was just going to go straight to university. To me, it didn't really feel like it was anything different. It just kind of felt like any other moving between institutions. Okay, we're done and now we're going to move on to the next level.

Participant 3 shared that the graduation was a formality of his transition to the IB program. According to this participant, the most important aspect at that time was attaining the IB diploma and passing the exam. He even added that he did not feel anything special at that time:

I can picture my college graduation a lot better. I can picture the robe, we were in the KeyArena, we did the walk and everything like that… this was high school. I'm trying to remember the emotions around it, and the experience around it. It was part of IB, we finished our tests, probably a month or so before school got out. Once we got finished with that, that was basically the end of our high school, just because that was basically what our entire high school was spent doing was preparing for these tests, so we already knew if we passed the tests or not, and I was never at risk for flunking and not graduating. I would consider my high school to have 60 people, not the 2000-something that it was. The only ones I saw on a daily basis were the 60 people who were in the IB, either full-time or part-time.

Yes, the entire school was there. We were all sitting with the people in the IB program. There, it was just kind of like a sea of red robes, I think for me, the graduation wasn't really the important part, it was the IB diploma, and passing that. When I was there, I was probably happy that I was graduating and it was all done, it was a big moment to graduation. But as far as feeling particularly special, I was surrounded by people who had done pretty much the same thing, and I guess we were all special, but I wouldn't necessarily say I felt it.

Minor theme 2: Feeling indifferent and isolated from the non-IB students. The second minor theme that followed was the feeling of being indifferent and isolated from the non-IB students. The theme had one occurrence or 20% of the sample; given that the theme had just one occurrence, further research is needed for validation. Participant 1 believed that he has always felt indifferent from the other students as they have always been separated during the regular school days. He added that the graduation was nothing special and went through a similar process and preparation as the rest of the students:

> I mean, we always felt kind of separate. I mean, essentially, we were housed in one corner of the school, and we would only ever take classes in that one corner of the school. We're going through this day to day activity, and then all of a sudden, it's one month until graduation and they're starting prep for walking and all that. They're calling in the entire senior graduating class to the auditorium to practice going up, so that there's no faux pas, no one tripping, no one doing any of that.

Thematic label 3: Overall IB program experiences. The third thematic label was the overall IB Program experiences of the participants. From the analysis, six themes were discovered. Majority of the participants reported that they were motivated from the active approach of the IB program. Meanwhile, other significant experiences shared were: having students who are all focused and goal-oriented; being open to learning and discovering knowledge at a deeper level; taking on new challenges in the different areas of life; having a passive learning approach; and using the program to prepare them for life in general. Table 4 contains the breakdown of the themes on the general IB program experiences of the five participants.

Table 4

Breakdown of the Themes on Overall IB Program Experiences

Themes	Number of Participants	Percentage of Participants
Being motivated from the active approach of the IB program	4	80%
Having students who are all focused and goal-oriented	3	60%
Being open to learning and discovering knowledge at a deeper level	3	60%
Taking on new challenges in the different areas of life	1	20%
Having a passive learning approach	1	20%
Using the program to prepare them for life in general	1	20%

Major theme 3: Being motivated from the active approach of the IB program. The

third major theme of the study was the experience of being motivated from the active and

rigorous approach of the IB program. The experience was shared by four or 80% of the

participants. Participant 1 described that the transition from a soft and passive school into an

active and rigorous academic approach was interesting for him. Such environment allowed him

to push himself to a higher level and explore the different learning approaches accordingly. He

also believed that with the high expectations of the program and the school from the IB students;

he was then motivated to working and achieving greater academic successes in the process of

completing his studies:

> This school has the highest record and the highest this and the highest that, and we expect
>
> great things from you. Moving from a soft, more passive advanced approach to a very
>
> active was very interesting to me… That's when I really had a more invested approach,
>
> okay now I can't slip up. I got to double down on ...

I would agree with that assessment. History at its core is the act of storytelling, the construction of a narrative. The IB program's methodology was important then because it allowed us to see the patterns in the narrative, putting us actually on the ship as it were. I think that having an overall academic that really just kind of complemented each other, being aggressive but not necessarily super active. Just kind of always passively in the background, keep pushing yourself, keep pushing yourself. Explore all these different philosophies and mindsets and traditions, and just bring it all together.

Participant 2 shared that the program that he participated in was more advanced when compared to the other programs of the different schools. With this, he concluded that students were also very much driven to perform their best and keep up with the expectations of the school and their educators. He also believed that the programs that he participated in allowed him to develop an increased drive and motivation; this was also the perception of the other students especially those outside if the program and community:

Well, the programs that I chose to participate in, that includes the Academy and that includes the IB program at Thomas Jefferson, I'd say they were more advanced than other schools in my community. That people who participated had more drive and motivation. I'd say that is the same opinion of my peers.

Furthermore, Participant 3 emphasized how the high standards of the program pushed the students to perform to the best of their abilities. He even shared that if he was enrolled in a normal school with slow-paced classes, he would not have excelled and learned as much as he did in the IB program. He added that the challenge and environment aided in his positive experience in the program:

The teachers, they had high standards, but they were hired with high standards as well, so for the most part from what I saw, they were good teachers and good people. There were times when it didn't seem like that, of course, but on the whole, I think that holds true. The people, the curriculum, just the fact that they pushed us a lot harder than a normal school, that definitely increased the trajectory of my academics, for the rest of my school career. If I had been in a normal school, taking slower classes and I didn't learn as much, I probably would have taken more time, had to take some of the basic classes, and I also mostly expanded my knowledge, vocabulary, work ethic, things like that. I feel like if I was in a normal school, just getting by on my own, not being challenged, then I might have carried that mentality with me for the rest of the while.

Finally, Participant 4 explained her experience in the IB program as a "good transition" coming from a traditional approach in her early years. Participant 4 believed that the IB program allowed and motivated her to perform her best in order to achieve the goals and platforms of the program. The structure of the program was a perfect fit for her as she enjoyed the challenge and the high standards that she had to live up to:

I actually took not a very traditional approach to high school. I went to kind of an experimental high school for freshman and sophomore year, and then I went straight into the IB program for the final years. It was a good transition for me. I really enjoyed schoolwork. I was very focused on getting everything done in time the way I wanted it to be done. You know, perfect grades, all that. So, the IB program was a really great fit for me. I enjoyed the structure. I liked the classes. I thought it was a lot more interesting than things that some of my friends who weren't in why IB program were doing. The only thing I would say is that it was a very small program, so it was kind of hard to interact with others outside of the program. I did enjoy it, and I felt like it was a good use of my time in high school.

Minor theme 1: Having students who are all focused and goal-oriented. The first minor theme that emerged was the experience of having students who are all focused and goal-oriented under the program. The experience was stated by three participants or 60% of the study. Participant 1 shared that the IB program requires students who are focused and motivated to excelling academically given the program structure and nature. The participant also added that from experience, students cannot be half-hearted and unsure when coming into the program. He believed that students should be 100% sure and motivated to stay in the program as the approach and environment would be difficult to achieve if the students were not fully committed:

I would definitely say that it does require someone who is, yes, advanced, but also is able to really rally all of their knowledge toward this goal. It's not something you can kind of half-ass. You just have to devote everything to that program in order to get the degree that you want.

I think the program is best for individuals who are very motivated and driven to really achieve great things and have good GPA and test scores. Someone who're more well-rounded than just, I'm really good at math and really good at writing and languages, but I don't really get English comprehension that well.

Meanwhile, Participant 2 stated that the program is composed of kids who have the same academic ethics and motivations. The participant added that the program was the foundation of the IB program students who have greater professional and career goals:

Probably was having that community of kids who are going through the same thing…

Because they had the same pressures of they might have to play an instrument or they

91

have to go and do all these community hours too. It was just a better understanding of

why we want to do this because we have similar goals in mind. It felt better than just

comparing ourselves to the other kids in high school who were just out playing and

partying and drag racing.

Honestly the drive came from the pressure, that's what I became accustomed to. It was

responding to pressure... I want to make sure that I have some form of a career, that I am

making a reliable paycheck. I mean a lot of standard typical things, you know? Be able to

buy my own home and that kind of success.

Participant 4 admitted that the program is not fit for all students. The participant reported

that the program's structure is rigorous and intensive; therefore, only the motivated and goal-

oriented individuals have a greater probability of being successful. Simply, Participant 4

believed that the programs are much specialized and not all students are fit for the academic

structure and approach:

I usually say it was a little bit more isolated than I think most of my friends, who went to

just a straight public school and didn't do specialized programs are. I say it was really

focused on preparing us for college and really learning a lot more things than I think a

basic high school program covers. It's maybe not for everyone, but it was really a good fit

for me and that overall I enjoyed it.

Minor theme 2: Being open to learning and discovering knowledge at a deeper level.

The second minor theme formed was being open to learning and discovering knowledge at a

deeper level and manner. The theme also received three occurrences or 60% of the participants.

Participant 1 stated that the program developed his deeper level of thinking and learning. He described the effect as the formation of an increased skepticism especially when taking in new knowledge and information:

Well, it's definitely resulted in a lot more skepticism. Skepticism in the sense of you always ask why. You never take information necessarily just at face value. You don't always actively ask whoever is presenting the information why, but you think about, is that information actually valid, does it fit within your knowledge of the greater context of the subject. If it doesn't, then yes, you raise questions about...

I think that in my world, it's definitely influenced how I collect and gather information, even if it's just day to day, like reading a newspaper. You read and are like, well, that's one argument for it, but let's pick apart why they are doing that subject. Let's look at their previous work. How is that influenced, how has their overall viewpoint on culture as a whole influenced their reporting of a subject.

Participant 4 explained that the program allowed her to develop a higher sense of thinking and learning. The participant stated that the different subjects under the IB program encouraged her to critically think in the process of completing an activity rather than just memorizing or assuming the lessons being taught:

I would say student learner. Just because to me, student scholar kind of confers a little bit more wisdom than I think I have as a student. I like to think that I'm continuously learning things and always looking for new things to figure out, so a scholar seems more like I have a lot of base knowledge that I wouldn't really assume.

I would say that it encourages us to actually think about what we're learning rather than just trying to get us to read and memorize things, which is what I saw outside of the program. I mean, there were definitely times, like in Theory of Knowledge, where I wasn't quite sure I was enjoying what I was doing, but most of the time, I did realize that

I was thinking critically about things that people my age outside the program probably

weren't doing, and I did appreciate that.

Participant 5 shared that he learns and acquires knowledge while analyzing them. For

this participant, the method thinking and learning from his Academy was developed and even

employed in his work today:

> I think my interest was maintained by my being detached from other students while still
>
> being part of the group. I was able to think about things. I think you called it *thinking*
>
> *about thinking* sometime this morning. I thought about that at the time and I am now
>
> thinking that that's what I did in school. I thought about thinking. I had my own invention
>
> of my school environment. By invention I mean I invented the school environment that
>
> suited me. I really wasn't part of anything and yet I was. I enjoyed moving around my
>
> own circle. My friends were myself and my conversations were whatever I want them to
>
> be. I'm beginning to think I went through the IB without ever being there. Now that's
>
> crazy but that's how I feel right now.
>
> But what is striking is that this is the first time I decided that school was thinking about
>
> thinking - to use your words. That's what I was doing. I was able to keep to myself while
>
> being part of a group and like both sides of that situation. Does that make sense? I mean,
>
> I guess my school is the foundation - that is Thomas Jefferson is the foundation - for how
>
> I operate today. I do a lot of analysis. When projects are discussed one of my jobs is to
>
> evaluate all options that relate to the project that are available as open source material. I
>
> don't speak with anyone when I do that I just do it, and think about it. I am kind of a go-
>
> to-guy for open source material that may affect new projects thereby saving internal

research costs or outside purchase costs. The only place I learned this was at Thomas Jefferson, or, the only place I practice it was at Thomas Jefferson.

Minor theme 3: Taking on new challenges in the different areas of life. The third minor theme was the learning from the program on having the ability to take on new challenges in the different areas and aspects of life. The theme received just one occurrence or 20% of the participants; this may need further research for validation. Participant 2 stated that the program allowed her to think critically and always challenge herself in the different situations she is faced with daily:

I challenged myself in different areas of my life. As a professional I'll take on projects that I am not completely comfortable with so I can learn new things. I like to continually learn on the creative portion of my life, so I'll take new dance classes or take new cooking classes, try new recipes and travel and meeting new people.

Minor theme 4: Having a passive learning approach. The fourth minor theme was the experience of having a passive learning approach. Similarly, the theme just had one occurrence. Participant 3 stated that as compared to the other IB students, his approach on his academics was more passive. He admitted that he just relied on his natural ability and skills to perform his educational responsibilities:

I just relied on my natural ability to do decently well, so I never really felt at risk of super bad grades, but I don't think I went the extra mile to make sure that I did well, and then going on after that, I think there might have been one of those aha moments, like you asked earlier, of that failure knocking you back, like a bad test or things like that, that kind of kick you into gear, and say okay, I'm actually going to try now.

Minor theme 5: Using the program to prepare them for life in general. The last minor theme was the utilization of the IB program in order to prepare the students for life after formal education. Again, the theme received just one occurrence. Participant 4 believed that the program was one of the main contributors to her success today. Participant 4 viewed the program as an experience that allowed her to develop as an individual and prepare her for life in general. For this participant, the program taught her to work harder and excel which she still uses in her professional career today:

> I would say it was a great place for me at the time. In high school, I was very, very shy, and it kind of gave me a way to focus on something other than socializing. I really did enjoy schoolwork, so that was also a good use of my time. I mean, I look back on it fondly, which I know some people in my program didn't really, because it was a lot of work. I do feel like it prepared me for life and school afterwards. No regrets. It prepared me for college, it prepared me for life, and I think it set me up to approach schoolwork in way that maybe I wouldn't have outside of the program in terms of actually appreciating what I was learning as opposed to just learning it, regurgitating it for a test, and then just forgetting it.
>
> I would say that it's really encouraged me to follow the path of hard work, if that makes any sense. I've always been a hard worker, but it definitely taught me the pathways for making sure that you're meeting deadlines, you're preparing yourself to complete a project each step of the way. Actually, that's very useful in my current job, because I have tons of deadlines and I have a lot of different things demanding my attention. Multitasking was definitely something I learned in the IB program. Yeah, I would actually say in my everyday life, I still use things that I learned from the IB program, just

96

because you have to do so much preparation and thinking and preparing for every single project in class. I mean, I still do that in my work life.

Thematic label 4: Education philosophy experiences from the IB program. The fourth thematic label was the discussion on the education philosophy perceptions and experiences from the IB program. Four themes were formed from the analysis. Majority of the participants believed that their schools had the main goal of equipping and preparing the IB students for College. Meanwhile, other important experiences were: creating well-rounded scholars; developing a broader array of knowledge over time; and one participant admitted to lacking the understanding of educational philosophy. Table 5 contains the breakdown of themes for the fourth thematic label.

Table 5

Breakdown of the Themes on Education Philosophy Experiences from the IB Program

Themes	Number of Participants	Percentage of Participants
Equipping and preparing IB students for College	2	40%
Creating well-rounded scholars	1	20%
Developing a broader array of knowledge over time	1	20%
Lacking the understanding of Educational Philosophy	1	20%

Major theme 4: Equipping and preparing IB students for college. The fourth major theme of the study was the perception and experience of seeing the educational philosophy of the schools as aimed to equipping and preparing the IB students for College. The theme was shared by two participants or 40% of the study. Participant 3 stated that the program's main goal with its rigorous approach was to prepare its students for College. The participant's experience highlighted that the program was vital in honing the minds and skills of the students and excel further in College:

I understood that their intentions were to be more rigorous to prepare us for college. That's actually pretty much what the academy and IB were for, was college prep. That was basically the intent. Their goal was that everyone who was in the programs would go to college, and that's what they were preparing you for.

Participant 4 echoed that there were numerous talks and orientations for college preparations under the program. In addition, the participant identified that the program offered a higher level of learning to better prepare them for College. Participant 4 also believed that the program was effective in successfully accomplishing the mission of College preparation and readiness for the students:

I mean, there was a lot of talk about preparing us for college, and I think that was mainly my takeaway from the whole thing is that they were really trying to prep us for higher learning and being prepared for everything that was to come.

Minor theme 1: Creating well-rounded scholars. The first minor theme of the study was the aim of creating of well-rounded scholars. The theme was reported by one participant or 20% of the sample. Participant 1 stated that the IB program has always presented its goal clearly. From experience, Participant 1 believed that the program had the main goal of developing and training well-rounded scholars:

Yeah, the International Baccalaureate program was very up front with what the goal was. It was they wanted to create extremely well-rounded scholars. It was assumed that you would all be going to university. This was just a stepping stone to get you into university. They also provided the carrot in the sense that there is the potential of getting college credit if you do well on these exams. The same would be true of advanced placement or if you did running start. All of those would get you prorated college credits.

The difference for me was that they were well-rounded. The whole concept as a scholar, as someone who can move seamlessly from conversing in Spanish to discussing the concept of slavery, the slavery revolution in Haiti back in 1840 whatever.

Minor theme 2: Developing a broader array of knowledge over time. The second minor theme of the fourth thematic label was the goal of developing a broader array of knowledge over time. Again, the theme just received one occurrence. Participant 2 shared how her knowledge continued to develop under the program. The IB program allowed her to meet new individuals which increased the opportunities for education and connections in the long run:

But my understanding grows each year since then. I continue to have a better understanding but I feel like I had a good grasp within the first year.

Because I have more knowledge to compare it to. I keep meeting more people and learning about their education and background and then I can plot similarities or differences and it just gives me more context.

Minor theme 3: Lacking the understanding of educational philosophy. The third minor theme was the experience of lacking the understanding of educational philosophy. Similarly, the theme received just one occurrence. Participant 5 questioned the need to understand and know the philosophy of the school. Participant 5 believed that it was not significant to know the mission and philosophy of the school: "Why am I supposed to understand the philosophy of the school?"

Thematic label 5: IB faculty experiences. The fifth thematic label was the IB Faculty Experiences. The thematic label had four themes. Majority of the participants reported that they had educators who were willing to help the students and impart their knowledge. Other important experiences with the faculty or teachers were: having the ability to freely discuss with the faculty; experiencing a conflict in academic instruction; and lacking interaction with teachers. Table 6 contains the breakdown of the themes on the IB faculty experiences shared by the IB program high school graduates.

Table 6

Breakdown of the Themes on IB Faculty Experiences

Themes	Number of Participants	Percentage of Participants
Willingness of educators to help and impart their knowledge	3	60%
Having the ability to freely discuss with the faculty	1	20%
Experiencing a conflict in academic instruction	1	20%
Lacking interaction with teachers	1	20%

Major theme 5: Willingness of educators to help and impart their knowledge. The fifth major theme of the study was the experience of having teachers and educators who were willing to help and impart their knowledge to their students. The theme was experienced by three or 60% of the participants. Participant 1 stated that from experience, majority of the IB program teachers and instructors were very much willing to share and impart their knowledge and skills to the students. Participant 1 believed that the teachers were successful in making the students feel valued and important:

Some teachers I was much closer to, like the history/English instructor I had in ninth and tenth grade. He was one of my first mentors and really saw in me a potential for instruction, and actually gave me opportunities to instruct the class on a couple of different occasions. I think if you're looking overall at my relationships with teachers, it could boiled down to that whole laissez-faire approach. We're here, here's the subject we're talking about. What is it? Why does it matter to us? What is it's greater importance to everything else? Your opinion matters as much as what I know and what my peers have said.

Participant 3 shared that he was fortunate to have developed and created good relationships with his teachers. The good relationships with the teachers allowed him to focus on his studies more and work harder.

I've been fortunate enough, for the most part, to have very good relationships with my teachers. I've always liked my teachers for the most part, been amicable with them. I've had friends who weren't, and I'd definitely say our experiences in school were a lot different. I liked my teachers generally, so I liked my classes. Other friends, teachers I loved, they hated. I guess it's a personal thing, but I really got along with them and I think that it definitely helps as far as education goes, because you'll pay more attention, you'll be less annoyed by homework, things like that.

Probably mostly the relationship with the teacher and working harder, and trying to focus more on things that I knew would help with that. I did definitely more work on the reviews and making sure that, like, the expectations were met, and things that were called out, learning from the previous gradings and things you got marked off on, and just kind of learning from that. Learning from mistakes.

Participant 4 echoed that the teachers were always willing to help the students under the program. Participant 4 stated that the teachers encouraged the students well and gave the proper advice for the students to boost their confidence and succeed in the future:

Oh, it was really good. I actually liked all of my teachers. They were always willing to give any kind of extra advice or help I might need. Very encouraging. Since it was such a small program, they knew all of us. They knew what each of us would need in order to succeed. I think I mentioned I was really quiet in high school, and my English teacher would often say, "You need to have more confidence. You're really good at this, you're really good at that. When you get up there, just think about that," for, you know, oral arguments and stuff. I would say, overall, very good.

Minor theme 1: Having the ability to freely discuss with the faculty. The first minor theme was the experience of having the ability to freely discuss with the faculty. Only one participant shared the experience or 20% of the study. Participant 1 stated that the program faculty gave him the freedom to have discussions about various subjects and topics. The participant shared that from experience, the discussions were very much open to the point that nothing was off limits as the teachers encouraged conversations on various subjects. Simply, Participant 1 believed that the conversational instruction was effective in building relationships with the faculty:

> I think overall, throughout the entire process, it's all based on the faculty. A lot of the faculty that I had with International Baccalaureate program did adopt that practice. My history instructor, psychology instructor, the English and art instructors, they all really adopted the approach of having this kind of conversational method of instruction. Having these open discussions about the subjects that we're talking about, where nothing is really off limits. You try to push the students through this method of really engaging with the core of the subject.

Minor theme 2: Experiencing a conflict in academic instruction. The second minor theme that emerged was the observation of experiencing a conflict in academic instruction. Again, only one participant shared the experience or 20% of the study. Participant 2 expressed that there were times when she observed that teachers would experience conflicts from wanting to teach one course structure but the state standards would require another. She described how there were academic conflicts inside the classroom:

> I think that is a defining characteristic of a good academic program, I wouldn't say it's everything. I know since the schools I went to were still public schools they had to adhere to standardized testing. That was always a conflict for the teachers because they knew how they wanted to teach us as an academic focused student group but they also had to shift from the desired course structure to meet Washington state standards. That was always a little tug-of-war in the classroom.

Minor theme 3: Lacking interaction with teachers. The third minor theme under the fifth thematic label was the experience of lacking interaction with the teachers. Again, only one participant shared the experience or 20% of the study. Participant 5 admitted that he had little to no interaction with the faculty. He added how he has always had 100% of the inputs from his work; without any help from the faculty:

> That depends on one's view I guess. Since I had little or no interaction with faculty, I suppose my personal input was practically 100%. I had all the input. The curriculum of the IB served as my platform to do what I wanted to do as long as I stayed inside their box. Now if the question addresses whether I gave input to the faculty to adjust course material, no. Never did that.

Thematic label 6: IB socialization experiences. The sixth thematic label was the discussion of the IB Socialization Experiences of the students. Three themes were discovered pertaining to the final thematic label of the study. Majority of the participants shared that the small environment allowed better connection with their friends. In addition, other noteworthy experiences were: instilling the freedom to express oneself; rigorous academic structure made it difficult to spend time with friends; and separating school and socialization. Table 7 contains the breakdown of the themes for the final thematic label.

Table 7

Breakdown of the Themes on IB Socialization Experiences

Themes	Number of Participants	Percentage of Participants
Small environment allowed better connection with friends	3	60%
Instilling the freedom to express oneself	1	20%
Rigorous academic structure made it difficult to spend time with friends	1	20%
Separating school and socialization	1	20%

Major theme 6: Small environment allowed better connection with friends. The sixth major theme discovered was that the small environment resulted to having better connection with their friends. Three participants were shared or 60% of the study. Participant 2 shared that the program has been a very important factor in developing connection and relationships with the other students. The participant indicated that the small environment allowed for her to understand different individuals better which she still practices in her profession today. She also expressed that the small environment was beneficial in meeting new individuals and developing close connections:

I would say very important... It's taught me who I get along with, who I don't get along with. I have learned more and more about people that I meet that I become a better judge of people whose personality will work well with my personality or not.

For example, in the beginning of our interview I mentioned the adolescent phase of middle school at the Academy. I wasn't a big fan of, I didn't like most of my classmates, I wasn't there for that, I didn't get enjoyment from the other students. Now that I've been out of school for so many years and met so many more people I have more context and I can compare the new personalities that I meet to some of those personalities from then. It was a typical clique kind of school and since I came in a year late I was one of the outsiders so I could never really find that niche or that home. But at the same time there was still a community all around because we were all in that school together so there was that shared pressure, that shared understanding of we need to succeed, we need to do well.

Participant 3 shared that with the small environment of the program, he was able to form close friendships. Participant 3 believed that the small environment is conducive in developing close friendships and relationships. In addition, the group works and projects were also some of the methods that developed interactions and connections between the students:

The friendships were great, because it was such a small environment, you got to know friends pretty well. Part of it, the shared challenge, because we all know it was tough. There was a general acceptance of the fact that we were doing pretty hard work, part of that, I think I mentioned earlier about like overcoming the hard work, part of that was also group effort... as there were a couple classes where we had group projects that we had to do, so then we kind of all got the shared experience that this is kind of hard on all of us.

Finally, Participant 4 highlighted that the program's small environment limited her to developing her socialization skills further. However, one advantage was the ability to get close to almost every member of the IB program:

In terms of the IB program, I would say it probably didn't have much effect on my socialization today, just because it did kind of enable me to be within a small group and not really go outside of that. I did become very close with everyone within the IB program. I shouldn't say everyone, but most of the people within the IB program because it was so small and you're seeing pretty much the same people every single class. I would say that was good and bad, just because it didn't force me to look outside of that and try to talk to other people, people outside the program even or just the larger group of people. I was kind of super shy in high school.

Minor theme 1: Instilling the freedom to express oneself. The first minor theme was the experience of being instilled with the freedom to express oneself to others. The theme received just one occurrence or 20% of the participants. Participant 1 stated that the program allowed him to develop the ability to be flexible around other individuals as he freely expresses oneself. In addition, the participant shared that the IB program provided an environment where he could share his perceptions and viewpoints to others openly:

Well, if you're taking it at face value, any sort of group educational system, any true school inherently begins that development of being essentially a microcosm of the world at large. You learn how to interact with people and how to tolerate viewpoints that you oppose or support viewpoints that you agree with. By its nature, the school did prepare me, but in terms of ... Looking at how my career path, being someone who's going into the academic world, I think that the schools I went to were extremely important in adapting me to this very specific social niche. This environment where you have a little more freedom to express your ideas with impunity. You're not being smacked down for your viewpoint, even if you disagree with it, or if someone more advanced disagrees with it.

Minor theme 2: Rigorous academic structure made it difficult to spend time with friends. The second minor theme pertained to the experience that the rigorous academic structure made it difficult to spend time with friends. Similarly, the theme received just one occurrence or 20% of the participants. Participant 3 admitted that with the program's strict and difficult structure, it became difficult for him to socialize outside the school and program. He added how it was hard to see friends especially when there were deadlines and requirements needed to be accomplished:

Probably vice versa. It was academically rigorous, and that made it harder to hang out with friends if you're doing homework. Especially for high school, 11th and 12th grade, living 25 minutes away made it a lot harder to hang out with anybody, because I was so far away from most of the people that went there, so that made it hard. I didn't have a car either, I wasn't one of the kids who was like I'm going to get my license at 16 and get a car and all that. That definitely impaired the social aspect of it, I would say.

Minor theme 3: Separating school and socialization. The third minor theme was the perception and experience of separating school and socialization. Again, the theme received just one occurrence or 20% of the participants. Participant 5 emphasized that he has always believed that school and socialization should be treated separately. He explained that the two aspects should be divided in terms of:

I have never made the connection between school and socialization in society. For me school was more literal. A training ground of sorts where I took new information to use for myself. I never think of school when I socialize. I understand I'm being too literal but I believe this interview will point that out when taken in total. I said before, I do not talk about school with my friends. The way I think has an effect on my socialization. I understand and accept that as a reality. However, I do not see that as structure in my day-to-day life. The two are separate as far as I am concerned.

Evaluation of Findings

This section contains the evaluation of findings in relation to the framework of the study. The main research question and its thematic categories should be discussed along with the major themes established under them. Again, the main research question was: What are IB students lived experiences regarding the transactional and transcendental /transpersonal synthesizing of their critical skills leading to higher order thinking during, and after graduating from, the IB Diploma Program?

From the findings of the phenomenological study, it was established that IB program students must have a strong educational understanding and viewpoint as well as the drive to endure the rigorous nature of the program. This was substantiated through the themes discovered using Moustakas' modified van Kaam method. The first thematic label which pertained to the early education experiences of the participants in which they found that they have always strived for academic excellence; and the second thematic label which was the experience of looking forward to finally graduating as an indicator of finally getting into and experiencing the IB program itself, give evidence to the educational principles of the IB program students. However, the main challenge as well as gap present within the current IB program is its ability to train both their educators and more so their students to move away from the traditional manner of teaching, learning, and thinking. Simply, as Doyon (2016) stated, transcendental phenomenology grasps the essence of transitioning away from the institutionalized actions and beliefs. Although the third major theme reported the experience of being motivated from the active approach of the IB program and the discovery through the fourth thematic label that the program's goal of equipping and preparing IB students for College was achieved. There is still a need to strengthen and modify the IB program's teaching approach to successfully produce "critical and innovative thinkers" (Smith & Morgan, 2010). In particular, the mandate was: "To develop to their fullest potential the powers of each individual to understand, to modify and to enjoy his or her environment, both inner and outer, in its physical, social, moral, aesthetic, and spiritual aspects" (Peterson, 2003, p. 33). This is because having an "active" method may be sufficient in motivating the students to perform well; however, it still undermines the supposed transcendent culture of the program. Furthermore, the fifth thematic label discussed the participants' experiences with the faculty wherein majority reported that the teachers had the willingness to help and impart their knowledge. Given this experience, participants expressed how these characteristics paved the way for them to develop the needed skills and knowledge to reach their potential/s as well as constantly think in a deeper and a more profound manner. Finally, the last thematic label pertained to the socialization experiences under the IB program. Participants reported that the small environment allowed better connection with friends. The finding then indicates that as the students are developing their skills and ability to activate their higher order of thinking; the program is successful in stimulating the social characteristics of their students. The next chapter should contain the complete discussion of the themes in relation to the literature of the study.

Summary

Chapter 4 of the study contained the findings from the analysis of the interviews with the five participants using Moustakas' (1994) modified van Kaam method. The purpose of this qualitative phenomenological research study was to understand the lived experience of IB students and why higher order thinking may not be achieved within the IB. Six major themes were discovered to address the main research question of: What are IB students lived experiences regarding the transactional and transcendental/transpersonal synthesizing of their critical skills leading to higher order thinking during, and after graduating from, the IB Diploma Program? In addition, minor themes were also established as the other noteworthy experiences of the participants under the IB program. From the findings, it can be inferred that IB program students must be academically inclined in order to fully grasp the essence and successfully attain the mandate and goals of the program. Furthermore, there is a need to reinforce the methods of learning and teaching to attain the transcendent culture of the program. The next chapter of the study should contain the discussion of the findings in relation to the literature, the recommendations, implications, and conclusions.

Chapter 5: Implications, Recommendations, and Conclusions

Chapter 5 deals with the implications of this study's research as well as recommendations which can be made as a result, and concludes with a summary of the study's essence. The chapter begins with an overview of the study, moves into the thematically-organized implications and springboards into recommendations for both practice and future research, concluding with a nuanced summary.

Overview of the Study

The problem statement was as follows: the enduring system of IB (International Baccalaureate) education represented as alternative education for gifted students is deficient in modes of learning, therefore undermining the IB program's goal of producing critical and innovative thinkers (Smith & Morgan, 2010), possibly due to a reliance on traditional educational approaches which exclude the transcendent culture of ephemeral inspiration (Cole et al., 2015; Grant, 2016). Although the IB is a respected program for gifted students worldwide, there are circumstances where gifted students do not reach the full potential of the IB education mandate: "To develop to their fullest potential the powers of each individual to understand, to modify and to enjoy his or her environment, both inner and outer, in its physical, social, moral, aesthetic, and spiritual aspects" (Peterson, 1987, p. 33). The onus is therefore on IB teaching professionals to be able to engage with IB students in such a way that the full possibilities of the IB program are realized, failing which the academic worth of the IB program and its students may be compromised.

Therefore, the purpose of this qualitative, phenomenological research study was to understand the lived experiences of former IB students and why higher order thinking may not be achieved within the IB, considering the wealth and depth of information provided by

111

phenomenology-based, qualitative reports. The study is framed by Empirical Phenomenology (EP) and Transcendental Phenomenology (TP) (Kordeš, 2016) and uses phenomenological reduction to answer the following Research Question: What are IB students' lived experiences regarding the transactional and transcendental /transpersonal synthesizing of their critical skills leading to higher order thinking during, and after graduating from, the IB Diploma Program? The following overarching themes emerged in the results section: Early Education Experiences, Graduation Experiences, Overall IB Program Experiences, Education Philosophy Experiences from the IB Program, IB Faculty Experiences and IB Socialization Experiences.

Thematic label 1: Early education experiences. Early education shapes learning trajectories and can instill practices and values at a young age. Information on IB students' early education experiences thus forms part of understanding processes of synthesizing critical life skills. Participants in this study overall indicated that the pursuit of academic excellence had been instilled in them since early childhood, with each expressing some level of familial encouragement and some expressing that they had been pushing for development of mind. A study by Drake et al. (2015) examined a Primary Years Program (PYP) designed to channel students into the IB system, giving the researchers insight into early education experiences. They looked at teachers, coordinators, and administrators perceived and applied transdisciplinary instructional and learning approaches, finding that students who underwent the program obtained higher academic achievement and gained more life and career skills compared to peers. Kitsantas and Miller's (2015) findings that the PYP influenced the students' levels of self-efficacy and self-regulation supports the argument that the this program is a stepping stone to the more intensive IB program, particularly for gifted students.

Conversely, Hemelt's (2015) similar study focusing on students from Michigan and North Carolina found discrepancies between data from the two states and could not conclude that the PYP program produced fixed results. Lochmiller et al. (2016) came to a similar conclusion in their study, saying that different stakeholders held different perceptions of how these programs affected them, negatively or positively. The minor theme identified in the present study, settling more contentedly with extra-curricular activities, supportively revealed that there are some gaps which can't be filled by an academic program alone. The main takeaway from the present study, under the theme of early education experiences, is that some graduates retrospectively felt that the influence of their families and developmental expectations of pathways to the IB program set them on a path towards the program.

Thematic label 2: Graduation experiences. The IB program is famed for its role in tertiary preparedness because of its reputation as a program which develops higher thinking (Culross & Tarver, 2011). The IB program was a natural next step towards preparing for a tertiary education for many of this study's participants, most of whom had looked forward to finally graduating. Assuming that the IB program is conducive to preparedness for college is accurate, according to Wolanin and Wade (2015), who studied the effects of the Middle Years IB Program (MYP), students enrolled in MYP could have higher levels of college-readiness as measured by at least one college-ready score on their college preparatory exam. In a study published by IB, Conley et al. (2014) revealed that high school students given the chance to take IB courses were more likely to do well in college academically and socially because they were so well adjusted. The present study's data further revealed certain levels of isolation that go along with being an IB student - there is a separate graduation ceremony for IB students from the rest

113

of the graduating class. This is an interesting illumination and one which warrants further study than this paper and Di Giorgio's (2010), which had a similar finding.

Thematic label 3: Overall IB program experiences. Capturing the collective experience of IB students is a difficult task, largely due to temporal, cultural and personal variation, as seen when comparing data from the present study with data from other, similar studies. However, it is a critical component of understanding how students' higher skills are developed. The literature review revealed a plethora of scholarship on critical thinking, with the National Council for Excellence in Critical Thinking (2016) drawing attention to its more metaphysical aspects. This core philosophical approach was shared by Brogan (2015), Polowczyk (2013), Richards (2015) and others. Conversely, scholars such as Jordan and Lande (2016) and Heinrich et al. (2015) emphasized the structural aspects of critical thinking. Therefore there seems to be a dichotomy between presciptivists and desciptivists, which depending on influences from popular theories at the time, fluctuates between the two as the leading schools of thought. This study, however, didn't yield much explicit information about critical thinking itself, with only Participants 2 and 4 revealing that they felt the IB program taught students to think critically rather than simply memorize information.

While the literature suggested a strong correlation between giftedness and academic achievement (No Child Left Behind Act, 2002; Reis et al, 2014) as well as critical thinking skills, this study's results tended towards a source of intrinsic and extrinsic motivation stemming from the IB program's high standards. This may be due to a movement away from the possibly elitist notion of gifted students, in an age of political correctness. These IB graduates stated that they found the program to have actively instilled a desire for learning and attaining deeper knowledge across a range of subjects. These findings are echoed by Bullock (2014), who remarked that IB learners were knowledgeable in that they were keen on developing deep knowledge of all the concepts, ideas, and issues that have local and global importance, largely due to the active teaching and learning approach of the IB.

The present study's participants felt that the IB program required students to have a high level of academic commitment and goal-orientation. In a study by Di Giorgio (2010), it was revealed that apart from the academic experience, parents chose to send their children to an IB program because they perceived it to offer a safe and challenging learning environment. The idea that the IB program offers a challenging environment to students was echoed by this study's participants. Another outcome of this study was that IB learning was not only an active experience: several participants felt that the IB program environment encouraged continuous reflection and other means of passive learning.

While some studies in the literature (e.g., Culross & Tarver, 2011) found that the workload of the IB program could be overwhelming for the students at first, this study did not have such a finding. A possible explanation for this may be that the participants, who were IB graduates, were nostalgic about the program and did not dwell much on its negatives.

The merits of the IB program are reflected in its increasing popularity, as noted by Per Plucker and Callahan (2014), although it has its competitors. Despite the continuous rise of IB programs, asides from this study, there is a shortage of literature which explores the relationship between IB and student learning attributes, including critical thinking and other higher-order thinking. The major contribution of the current study in this regard is a retrospective, student-informed insight into the IB program and how it facilitates higher skills.

Thematic label 4: Education philosophy experiences from the IB program. The nature of this study and the field in which it is positioned entailed using a deliberate philosophical lens through which to view the participants and future-forging academic experiences. Such a strategy captured the more abstract aspects of the study, including the notions of College preparedness and Educational Philosophy. Knowles et al. (2014) highlighted the role of critical thinking as a structural device of the IB, in that it marked a transition from pedagogy in the earlier years to andragogy in later years. In this case, critical thinking was considered a strategy as opposed to an outcome. This sentiment resonated with those of this study's participants: they viewed the IB as a major stepping stone towards College preparedness.

Another study which highlighted the College pathway status of IB (as well as AP) was that of Park et al. (2014). It was assumed that just by participating in these programs, universities, administrators, and even families were more likely to think highly of the students. The authors systematically evaluated the experiences of the students who participated in these pathway programs themselves to see if what universities, administrators, and families perceive the students learn and acquire through these programs were the same as the actual experiences of the students, deducing that the experience can be affected by peer relationships, teacher-student relationships, perceptions of success, self-image, and perceived preparation for the future experienced and fostered by these programs. Beckwitt, Van Kamp, and Carter (2015) explored student perceptions of the program in a different light: they found that DP students often perceived themselves as having higher key nonacademic attributes (such as cultural sensitivity) because of their learning experience. One can deduce that these nonacademic attributes would shape student experiences of educational philosophy.

In a slightly different vein, Ateskan et al. (2015) looked at the impact of the IB DP. They found that it was a better program for college preparedness than the Turkish Ministry's National Education Program, and additionally correlated with higher graduation rates. Bergeron's (2015) study also evaluated the DP's effects, specifically on the rate of enrollment in college and post-secondary outcomes. Similar to Ateskan et al., the finding was that IB DP could have a positive impact on college enrollment after high school as well as on graduation rates. Wright (2015) went a step further and found that IB programs have lasting effects beyond college readiness and graduation, extending beyond academic success to general success in life.

The present study's participants also gave insight into the idea of the well-rounded student and how IB facilitates ever-growing knowledge, although there was a lack of understanding of the concept of Educational Philosophy since participants did not see its relevance to them. (This is matter-of-fact the case based on the interviews) In the sense of better understanding how students perceive the transactional and transcendental /transpersonal synthesizing of their critical skills, this study is pioneering.

Thematic label 5: IB faculty experiences. Student-faculty relations within the IB program have largely been unexplored according to the literature, leaving a chasm in knowledge of and surrounding the IB program. The majority of participants in a study by Thomas (2011) reported that their IB teachers did display a willingness to help them and to impart knowledge and that good relationships between students and teachers were a source of motivation and student confidence. Some participants felt that they could freely discuss many topics with teachers, with one even finding that the state-mandated syllabus limited the learning experience despite teachers displaying the desire to extend knowledge. Thomas (2011) concluded that educators across disciplines could bolster student-faculty relations by should actively imparting critical thinking skills to their students. To this end, he helpfully listed various critical thinking skills and methods for their instruction. The present study therefore gives important insight into faculty experiences within the IB program, an area that has been largely ignored by other scholars.

Thematic label 6: IB socialization experiences. There are varying accounts of the IB's impact on socialization. The majority of participants in this study reported that the small environment was conducive to better, closer friend relationships and to self-expression. However, the program could be construed as creating a social bubble because of its exclusivity and an impeder of social time because of its rigorous academic demands. MacRaild's (2015) finding in this regard was that the IB program had profound effects on the social values being acquired by the students through their history education. Some examples are: students learned how to be more independent and critical in encountering, interpreting, and comprehending history. One participant in the present study drew a distinction between school and socialization, saying he believed they should be treated separately, which is at odds with other data. Most studies around the IB program focus on the program's academic impact (Peterson, 2003); therefore, this study has been able to contribute to a better understanding of IB's impact on the social lives of students. This insight provides a richer, more holistic understanding of IB experiences, which could contribute to higher skills synthesis.

Limitations

As initially identified in Chapter 3, there are several, possible limitations. Sample size is often a limiting consideration due to questionable generalizability, however in this case, the sample size was not a barrier as it met the typical phenomenology study size considered satisfactory for thematic development leading to saturation (Creswell, 2014; Moustakas, 1994; Silverman, 2013). Although phenomenology itself is not without its pitfalls, the studied underpinnings of qualitative research were brought to bear through the lived experiences of the subjects in this case. Identified issues with phenomenological research include descriptive versus interpretive analysis, objective versus subjective, and participant voice versus researcher voice (Shi, 2011). It is possible to negate the possibility of subjective, researcher-voiced analysis through either triangulation or stratified revisiting of the subject in a phenomenological reduction, as has been the case in this study. The choice of using phenomenological reduction in this study can be justified by the following, eloquent quote: "The world of nature, as explored by the natural scientist, does not 'mean' anything to the molecules, atoms and electrons. But the observational field of the social scientist – social reality – has a specific meaning and reference structure for the human beings living, acting and thinking within it" (Schutz, 1962, p. 59).

In addition, during the data collection process and the write-up of results it emerged that there were terms employed that could be construed as obtuse. Where possible, the researcher clarified these terms so as not to obscure meaning. The researcher also realized that the particular participants chosen, through purposeful selection from one student body, would have a major impact on conclusions drawn. This realization meant that exact findings from this participant group likely could not be replicated with another group, although the findings were rich in nature and gave a true snapshot into some IB graduates' lived experiences. The snapshot nature of the research could also be seen as limiting in that the experiences leading up to the interview process and the events succeeding it could not be captured.

The assessment instrument used was an interview guide of 22 questions, which informed open-ended conversational interviews. The informal nature of these types of interviews limited the researcher insofar as tangential conversations to the research question could dominate the data, but they are useful in that participants may be less likely to be coerced into rigid conversations and so feel freer to express their true thoughts. In addition, procedures were put into place so as to mitigate against some of the pitfalls of phenomenological reduction: a great deal of time was spent on thematic overlays based on repetitive examination of underlying linguistic characteristics, leading to important and interesting insights for all stakeholders. Moustakas (1995) captured the value of this process, stating that the associated multi-layered perceptions become transcendental because they uncover the individuality from which everything presents meaning.

Implications

The Research Question of this study was: What are IB students' lived experiences regarding the transactional and transcendental /transpersonal synthesizing of their critical skills leading to higher order thinking during, and after graduating from, the IB Diploma Program? The implications of this study have been organized thematically, that is: sample, methodology, research design and findings.

Sample. Although the sample size was not determined to be a significant limitation on this study, it does have implications for this and for future research. This study has shown it is possible to extract rich, multi-layered meaning from a relatively small number of participants. Additionally, the selection process around the sample provides insight into ethical, research-backed procedures which can be used for future research.

Methodology. The implications of the use of Phenomenological Reduction in a study about the IB program are significant: much of the literature around the IB is grounded in other social sciences (psychology, development, education) whereas this one has taken a philosophical approach and used a method associated with philosophy. This study has shown that it is possible to look at topics through the lens of a discipline not routinely associated with said topics, which can work to the favor of the researcher by offering a different and fresh perspective. In this case, there have been many studies of the IB but not within the field of philosophy. Bracketing, a term associated with phenomenology, ensures a systematic layering of understanding while intentionality aims to voluntarily awaken and sustain the force of conceptual cognition.

Research design. Selection of the research participants was accomplished through purposeful sampling, guided by a defined set of parameters. Just as the assessment instruments are deliberately based on nascent trends in the literature, so too were the procedures designed to galvanize the study and produce the deepest, clearest understanding possible of the data. The methodical revisitation of the data in particular is a useful strategy for any qualitative research, since it mitigates some of the risks of subjectivity.

Findings. The main themes drawn from the literature were: gifted students, critical thinking, taxonomy, evolution of transcendental phenomenology, teacher relations in the IB system and socialization and culture. This study extended knowledge in the areas of: early education experiences, graduate experiences, overall IB program experiences, education philosophy experiences, IB faculty experiences and IB socialization experiences. While there certainly overlaps between the two, this study provided deep insight into students' lived experiences, translating into knowledge about how transcendental teaching and learning within the IB program lead to the development of higher skills. The researcher found that this process transcended just the academic. The problem statement (summarized as: The renowned IB program possibly falls short of its goals of producing critical thinkers because of a monolithic approach which excludes transcendental education) is addressed in that the IB program is revealed to be more multifaceted than previously thought. This realization could lead to a more nuanced approach to the IB program in future, thus increasing its potential to produce thinking students. Within the themes emerging from this study, there are further implications.

Early education experiences. Although the IB has a PYP (Primary Years Program), some of the findings of this study could assist in improving it. Participants revealed that they had felt a sense of academic pressure from an early age, in some cases from parents who had not completed their schooling, and that extracurricular activities were helpful in managing stress. There is therefore scope for the IB to provide better support for its PYP students and to look at placing a greater emphasis on the non-academic component of the program.

Graduation experiences. This study's participants overall looked forward to graduating but some felt isolated from their non-IB peers. The recommendation is therefore that the IB either connects graduating students within a particular area (so as to give them a sense of belonging to a bigger group) or integrate the IB ceremony within the schools' core graduation.

Overall IB program experiences. Participants reported having enjoyed the active and community approaches of the IB program. The IB could consider including more active elements in the program so as to better engage students while concentrating on making them feel like part of a community. Due to the demanding nature of the IB program, it seems that belonging to a community is at the core of students being able to cope. Additionally, the knowledge-seeking aspect of the IB students stood out amongst this study's participants: they sometimes felt limited by the program's rigid structure and adherence to syllabus. The program could therefore benefit from innovative ways of extending knowledge, without detracting from the program's core requirements. For the purposes of College preparedness and program registrations, it would be worth emphasizing that the IB produces students who are skilled across disciplines and who constantly seek further knowledge.

IB faculty experiences. Participants in this study reported overall good relations with the teachers, disclosing how meaningful those relationships were in their performance and wellbeing. The recommendation is therefore that the IB invests further in IB educators and ensures that the high standard of teaching continues.

Student socialization experiences. Across themes, the study's participants highlighted the role of socialization in their program experience. Due to the exclusive nature of the IB program, there is a great need for the creation and promotion of social spaces in which IB students can socialize and develop support systems. This could be facilitated through frequent IB social events, mentoring systems or relationship-building workshops.

At a student level, the study's findings enable a better understanding of the IB program and how students can make the most of it. Families are able to make better informed choices about the selection of an extension program, being more familiar with the dynamics of the IB. As an organization, the IB can take this study's findings and use them to improve and refine the program (the PYP and the IB itself) in such a way that it achieves its goals and continues to be seen as the pinnacle of high school education. Academics are able to look at the program as well as the idea of transcendental education with a renewed focus.

Recommendations for Practice

Practically speaking, there are a number of organizations and groups who may be interested in this study and its findings. The IB would benefit from engaging with this study, as would other practitioners and organizations in the gifted education space. The findings reveal a side of the IB program not previously considered and, if applied correctly, could result in an improved version of the program with a greater number of students emerging with critical thinking skills. The following recommendations can therefore be made, based on the study's implications: the IB could tailor their early education programs in such a way that more importance is placed on extra-curricular activities, the IB could look at ways to improve

123

students' graduation experiences and the IB could use the insights from the present study's participants to improve students' overall experiences of the IB program. It is also recommended that the IB organization further emphasize the capacity of the program to develop well-rounded students, thereby attracting parents to the IB as a possible program for their children. Lastly, the IB could improve relations between student and faculty as well as create an environment conducive to student socialization.

Recommendations for Future Research

Researchers interested in this area of study can benefit from this study. Areas for consideration include: the framework, the findings and the implications. This study is framed by phenomenology, with phenomenological reduction used as the methodology. Phenomenology and its tools have proved to be advantageous in studies pertaining to lived experiences, particularly when a small sample is used. It is recommended that future researchers consider phenomenology which, although traditionally a philosophical concept, could be applied across disciplines.

The findings of this study should pave the way for future research, guided by the thematic areas. This study used an informal interview structure to gather data but, based on future researchers' areas of interest, more structured methods could be applied to gather data on a particular theme. Furthermore, there is scope for future researchers to build on the research question of this study by either phrasing it differently (for example, looking at specific transcendental learning strategies within the IB) or selecting a different sample from another population (for example, a sample of IB graduate from another country or perhaps a different population within the United States of America). The next logical step for future researchers would be to look at how the IB program could better incorporate transcendental learning in order to further their agenda. A study along these lines would galvanize the present study's findings and pave the way for practical, actionable educational solutions.

The implication that researchers should look beyond just the academic is significant for future research. The literature suggests that the IB program has traditionally been explored from multiple perspectives informed by its academic prowess. There are potentially many different facets of the IB program which could be explored in future research.

Conclusions

This study has addressed the following problem statement: the enduring system of IB education represented as alternative education for gifted students is deficient in modes of learning, therefore undermining the IB program's goal of producing critical and innovative thinkers (Smith & Morgan, 2010), possibly due to a reliance on traditional educational approaches which exclude the transcendent culture of ephemeral inspiration (Cole, et al., 2015; Grant, 2016). Although IB is a respected program for gifted students worldwide, there are circumstances where gifted students do not reach the full potential of the IB education mandate. The onus is therefore on IB teaching professionals to be able to engage with IB students in such a way that the full possibilities of the IB program are realized. The study was guided by the Research Question: What are IB students' lived experiences regarding the transactional and transcendental /transpersonal synthesizing of their critical skills leading to higher order thinking during, and after graduating from, the IB Diploma Program?

The study found that IB students' lived experiences were rich and varied, leading to the conclusion that there were many factors leading to the achievement of higher order thinking within the scope of the program. Previous literature had focused on the academic side of the IB program but this study looked beyond. In the informal, semi-structured interviews participants had the freedom to share anecdotes about their experiences of the IB program and retrospectively consider how the program contributed to their tertiary and life preparedness. The purpose of this qualitative, phenomenological research study, as identified in the very beginning of the study, has therefore carried throughout: to understand the lived experience of IB students and why higher order thinking may not be achieved within the IB, considering the wealth and depth of information provided by phenomenology-based, qualitative reports (Moustakas, 1995). The selection of methodology and the research design as a whole have enabled a captivating study with new insights and fresh perspectives into transcendental education, honing in on critical thinking.

The study's implications have been considered from a variety of perspectives. Both practical and theoretical implications have emerged and recommendations made based on these. This study has therefore been able to make significant contributions to academia as well as to the IB system and its networks. Having recapped the main points and contributions, Chapter 5 concludes this study.

References

Abadzi, H., Martelli, M., & Primativo, S. (2014). *Explorations of creativity: A review for educators and policy makers.* Doha, Qatar: Qatar Foundation International.

Agassi, J. (2015). Einstein's philosophy politely shelved. *Philosophy of the Social Sciences, 45*(4/5), 515. doi:10.1177/0048393115571251

Akmansoy, V., & Kartal, S. (2014). Chaos Theory and its application to education: Mehmet Akif Ersoy University Case. *Educational Sciences: Theory and Practice, 14*(2), 510-518. Retrieved from http://www.edam.com.tr/estp.asp

Aktas, B. C., & Guven, M. (2015). Comparison of Secondary Education Mother Tongue Teaching Courses in the International Baccalaureate Program with the National Program in terms of Critical Thinking. *Educational Sciences: Theory & Practice, 15*(1), 99-123. doi:10.12738/estp.2015.1.2286

Altintas, E., & Ilgün, S. (2015). The perception of gifted students' parents about the term of giftedness. *Educational Research and Reviews, 10*(5), 654-659. Retrieved from http://www.academicjournals.org/journal/ERR

Androutsopoulou, A. (2015). Moments of meaning: Identifying inner voices in the autobiographical texts of 'Mark'. *Qualitative Psychology, 2*(2), 130-146. doi:10.1037/qup0000028

An Interview with George Yancy, Professor of Philosophy, Duquesne University. (2015). Aegis: The Otterbein Humanities Journal, 15.

Ateşkan, A., Onur, J., Sagun, S., Sands, M., & Çorlu, M. S. (2015). *Alignment between the DP and MoNEP in Turkey and the effects of these programmes on the achievement and development of university students.* Retrieved from http://www.ibo.org/globalassets/publications/ib-research/dp/turkey-postsecondary-study-report-en.pdf

Bahadır, E. (2016). Metaphorical perceptions of geometrical concepts by secondary school students identified as gifted and identified as non-gifted. *International Online Journal of Educational Sciences, 8*(1), 118-137. doi:10.15345/iojes.2016.01.011

Bailey, T., Jaggars, S. S., & Jenkins, D. (2015*). Implementing guided pathways at Miami Dade College: A case study* (Dissertation). Miami, FL: Community College Research Center, Teachers College, Columbia University.

Bailey, T., Jaggars, S. S., Jenkins, D., & Columbia University, C. C. (2015). What we know about guided pathways: Helping students to complete programs faster. research overview. Ithaca, NY: Community College Research Center, Teachers College, Columbia University.

Barclay, M. W. (2000). The inadvertent emergence of a phenomenological perspective in the philosophy of cognitive psychology and psychoanalytic developmental psychology. *Journal Of Theoretical And Philosophical Psychology, 20*(2), 140-166. doi:10.1037/h0091207

Baudson, T. G., & Preckel, F. (2013). Teachers' implicit personality theories about the gifted: An experimental approach. *School Psychology Quarterly, 28*(1), 37-46. doi:10.1037/spq0000011

Baudson, T. G., & Preckel, F. (2016). Teachers' conceptions of gifted and average-ability students on achievement-relevant dimensions. *Gifted Child Quarterly, 60*(3), 212. doi:10.1177/0016986216647115

Bayne, T., & Montague, M. (2011). *Cognitive phenomenology.* New York, NY: Oxford University Press on Demand.

Beaven, E. K. (2011). *Exploring things seen and unseen: Students speak of Waldorf education* (Doctoral Dissertation, University of California). (3474344)

Beavan, V. (2011). Towards a definition of "hearing voices": A phenomenological approach. *Psychosis, 3*(1), 63-73. doi:10.1080/17522431003615622

Beckwitt, A., Van Camp, D., & Carter, J. (2015). *International Baccalaureate implementation study: Examination of district-wide implementation in the US.* Germantown, MD: Asher Consulting.

Béneker, T., van Dis, H., & van Middelkoop, D. (2014). World-mindedness of students and their geography education at international (IB-DP) and regular schools in the Netherlands. *International Journal of Development Education and Global Learning, 6*(3), 5-30. Retrieved from http://www.ingentaconnect.com/content/ioep/ijdegl;jsessionid=21xlpxgd522uj.alice

Benny, N., & Blonder, R. (2016). Factors that promote/inhibit teaching gifted students in a regular class: Results from a professional development program for chemistry teachers. *Education Research International, 2016.*

Bensley, D. A., Rainey, C., Murtagh, M. P., Flinn, J. A., Maschiocchi, C., Bernhardt, P. C., & Kuehne, S. (2016). Closing the assessment loop on critical thinking: The challenges of multidimensional testing and low test-taking motivation. *Thinking Skills and Creativity, 21*(2), 158-168.

Bergeron, P. H. (2015). *Antebellum politics in Tennessee.* Appalachia, KY: University Press of Kentucky.

Bishop, F. L., & Yardley, L. (2007). Qualitative assessment. In *Cambridge Handbook of psychology, health, and medicine.* Cambridge, UK: Cambridge University Press.

Blake, J., & Illingworth, S. (2015). Interactive and interdisciplinary student work: A facilitative methodology to encourage lifelong learning. *Widening Participation & Lifelong Learning, 17*(2), 108-118. doi:10.5456/WPLL.17.2SI.107

Blau, D., Bach, L., Scott, M., & Rubin, S. (2013). Clark Moustakas (1923–2012): Scholar, teacher, colleague and friend. *The Humanistic Psychologist, 41*(1), 97-99. doi:10.1080/08873267.2013.752695

Bloomberg, L. D., & Volpe, M. F. (2012). *Completing your qualitative dissertation: A roadmap from beginning to end.* Thousand Oaks, CA: Sage.

Bowman-Perrott, L., deMarín, S., Mahadevan, L., & Etchells, M. (2016). Assessing the Academic, Social, and Language Production Outcomes of English Language Learners Engaged in Peer Tutoring: A Systematic Review. *Education & Treatment of Children, 39*(3), 359-388.

Brogan, W. (2005). *Heidegger and Aristotle: The twofoldness of Being.* Albany, NY: State University of New York Press.

Brook, A. (2016). Is it possible to be a phenomenological Thomist? An investigation of the notions of esse and esse commune. *New Blackfriars, 97*(1067), 93-110. doi:10.1111/nbfr.12000

Brooks, D. (2016, April 15). What is inspiration? *New York Times,* p. A25.

Budsankom, P., Sawangboon, T., Damrongpanit, S., & Chuensirimongkol, J. (2015). Factors affecting higher order thinking skills of students: A meta-analytic structural equation modeling study. *Educational Research and Reviews, 10*(19), 2639-2652. Retrieved from http://www.academicjournals.org/journal/ERR

Bullock, K. (2011). International Baccalaureate learner profile: Literature review. Cardiff, UK. *International Baccalaureate Organization. Retrieved from the International Baccalaureate Organization website: www. ibo. org/research/resources/documents/LPLitReview_final. pdf.*

Butvilas, T. (2014). Openness within adoption: Challenges for child's psychosocial development and self-identity. *Global Journal of Psychology Research, 4*(1), 22-28. Retrieved from http://www.world-education-center.org/index.php/gjpr

Cahill, K. M. (2014). Quietism or description; McDowell in dispute with Deryfus. *Review of Metaphysics, 68*(2), 395-409. Retrieved from http://www.reviewofmetaphysics.org/index.php

Callahan, C. M., & Hertzberg-Davis, H. L. (Eds.). (2012). *Fundamentals of gifted education: Considering multiple perspectives.* New York, NY: Routledge.

Campàs, O. (2016). A toolbox to explore the mechanics of living embryonic tissues. *Seminars in Cell and Developmental Biology.* doi:10.1016/j.semcdb.2016.03.011

Card, D., & Giuliano, L. (2014). *Does gifted education work? For which students?* (No. w20453). Cambridge, MA: National Bureau of Economic Research.

Card, D., & Giuliano, L. (2015). *Can universal screening increase the representation of low income and minority students in gifted education?* (No. w21519). Cambridge, MA: National Bureau of Economic Research.

Cargas, S. (2016). Honoring controversy: Using real-world problems to teach critical thinking in honors courses. *Honors in Practice, 12*(1), 123-137.

Castro, P., Lundgren, U., & Woodin, J. (2015). International Mindedness through the looking glass: Reflections on a concept. *Journal Of Research In International Education, 14*(3), 187. doi:10.1177/1475240915614202

Celuch, K., Kozlenkova, I., & Black, G. (2010). An exploration of self-efficacy as a mediator of skill beliefs and student self-identity as a critical thinker. *Marketing Education Review, 20*(3), 70-80. doi:10.2753/MER1052-8008200306

Chaipichit, D., Jantharajit, N., & Chookhampaeng, S. (2015). Development of learning management model based on constructivist theory and reasoning strategies for enhancing the critical thinking of secondary students. *Educational Research and Reviews, 10*(16), 2324-2330. doi:10.5897/ERR2015.2193

Charmaz, K. (2006). *Constructing grounded theory: A practical guide through qualitative analysis.* Thousand Oaks, CA: Sage.

Chatlos, J. (2015). *The relationship of middle years program teachers' beliefs and practice to the International Baccalaureate Learner Profile. International Baccalaureate.* Retrieved from http://www.ibo.org/contentassets/4ccc99665bc04f3686957ee197c13855/myp-teachers-and-learner-profile-executive-summary-en.pdf

Chen, W. (2015). Relationships between perceived parenting behaviors and academic achievement among high school students in International Baccalaureate (IB) Programs: A comparison of Asian American and White Students (Doctoral dissertation, University of South Florida).

Chomsky, N., & Barsamian, D. (2015). *Propaganda and the public mind: Conversations with Noam Chomsky.* Chicago, IL: Haymarket.

Claxton, G. (2012). Turning thinking on its head: How bodies make up their minds. *Thinking Skills And Creativity, 7*(1), 78-84. doi:10.1016/j.tsc.2012.03.004

Clinkenbeard, P. R. (2012). Motivation and gifted students: Implications of theory and research. *Psychology in the Schools, 49*(7), 622-630. Retrieved from http://onlinelibrary.wiley.com/journal/10.1002/(ISSN)1520-6807

Cole, D. R., Ullman, J., Gannon, S., & Rooney, P. (2015). Critical thinking skills in the International Baccalaureate's "Theory of Knowledge" subject: Findings from an Australian study. *Australian Journal of Education, 59*(3), 247. doi:10.1177/0004944115603529

Coleman, L. J., Micko, K. J., & Cross, T. L. (2015). Twenty-five years of research on the lived experience of being gifted in school. *Journal for the Education of the Gifted, 38*(4), 358. doi:10.1177/0162353215607322

Conley, D., McGaughy, C., Davis-Molin, W., Farkas, R., & Fukuda, E. (2014). *International Baccalaureate Diploma Programme: Examining college readiness.* Eugene, OR: The Education Policy Improvement Center.

Conrad, B., Moroye, C. M., & Uhrmacher, P. B. (2015). Curriculum disruption: A vision for new practices in teaching and learning. *Current Issues in Education, 18*(3), 1-19. Retrieved from https://cie.asu.edu/ojs/index.php/cieatasu

Cooper, C. R. (1995). Integrating gifted education into the total school curriculum. *School Administrator, 52*(1), 8-8. Retrieved from http://www.aasa.org/SchoolAdministrator.aspx

Corbin, J., & Strauss, A. (2008*). Basics of qualitative research: Techniques and procedures for developing grounded theory* (3rd ed.). Thousand Oaks, CA: Sage.

Corlu, M. (2014). Which preparatory curriculum for the International Baccalaureate Diploma Programme is best? The challenge for international schools with regard to mathematics and science. *International Review of Education, 60*(6), 793-801. doi:10.1007/s11159-014-9446-9

Corry, R. (2015). Retrocausal models for EPR. *Studies in History and Philosophy of Modern Physics,* 491-9. doi:10.1016/j.shpsb.2014.11.001

Crease, R. P., & Goldhaber, A. S. (2014). *The quantum moment: How Planck, Bohr, Einstein, and Heisenberg taught us to love uncertainty.* New York, NY: WW Norton & Company.

Cross, J. R., Cross, T. L., & Finch, H. (2010). Maximizing student potential versus building community: An exploration of right-wing authoritarianism, social dominance orientation, and preferred practice among supporters of gifted education. *Roeper Review, 32*(4), 235-248. doi:10.1080/02783193.2010.508155

Cross, T. L., Stewart, R. A., & Coleman, L. J. (2003). Phenomenology and its implications for gifted studies research: Investigating the lebenswelt of academically gifted students attending an elementary magnet school. *Journal for the Education of the Gifted, 26*(3), 201-220. doi:10.1177/016235320302600304

Creswell, J. W. (2014). *Research design.* Thousand Oaks, CA: Sage.

Culross, R., & Tarver, E. (2011). A summary of research on the International Baccalaureate Diploma Programme: Perspectives of students, teachers, and university admissions offices in the USA. *Journal of Research in International Education, 10*(3), 231-243. doi:10.1177/1475240911422139

Dando, P. (2016). Traditional literacy and critical thinking. *Knowledge Quest, 44*(5), 8-12. Retrieved from http://knowledgequest.aasl.org/

Davaslıgil, Ü. (2000). *Intercultural aspect of creativity: Challenges and barriers-the case in Turkey.* Istanbul, Turkey: Istanbul University.

Denzin, N. K., & Lincoln, Y. S. (2011). *The Sage handbook of qualitative research.* Thousand Oaks, CA: Sage.

Desmidt, S. (2016). The Relevance of Mission Statements: Analysing the antecedents of perceived message quality and its relationship to employee mission engagement. *Public Management Review, 18*(6), 894-917. doi:10.1080/14719037.2015.1051573

Di Giorgio, C. (2010). Choices of students, parents, and teachers and their effects on schools and communities: A case study of a new enriched high school program. *Journal of School Choice, 4*(3), 278-292. doi:10.1080/15582159.2010.504107

Din, A. M. (2016). Quantum mechanical reality according to Copenhagen 2.0. *International Journal of Modern Physics A: Particles & Fields; Gravitation; Cosmology; Nuclear Physics, 31*(14/15), 1. doi:10.1142/S0217751X16300143

Diprose, R., & Reynolds, J. (2009). *Merleau-Ponty: Key concepts.* Stocksfield, UK: Acumen.

Diprose, R., & Reynolds, J. (2014). *Merleau-Ponty: Key concepts.* New York, NY: Routledge.

Donovan M. S., Cross C. T. (Eds.). (2002). *Minority students in special and gifted education.* Washington, DC: National Academies Press.

Doyon, M. (2016). Intentionality and normativity. *Philosophy Today.* doi:10.5840/philtoday2016113105

Drake, J. (2002). The academic brand of aphasia: Where postmodernism and the science wars came from. *Knowledge, Technology & Policy, 15*(1/2), 13. Retrieved from http://link.springer.com/journal/12130

Drake, S. M., Savage, M. J., Reid, J. L., Bernard, M. L., & Beres, J. (2015*). An exploration of the policy and practice of transdisciplinary in the IB PYP Programme.* Retrieved from http://www.ibo.org/globalassets/publications/ib-research/pyp/an-exploration-of-the-policy-and-practice-of-transdisciplinarity-in-the-pyp-final-report.pdf

Dyck, C. W. (2015). Beyond the paralogisms: The proofs of immortality in the lectures on metaphysics. In R. Clewis (Ed.), *Reading Kant's lectures* (pp. 115-134). Berlin, Germany: De Gruyter. doi:10.1515/9783110345339-012

Eichinger, R., & Lombardo, M. (2004). *FYI for your improvement: A guide for development and coaching.* New York, NY: Lominger Press.

Erwin, J. O., & Worrell, F. C. (2012). Assessment practices and the underrepresentation of minority students in gifted and talented education. *Journal of Psychoeducational Assessment, 30*(1), 74-87. Retrieved from http://jpa.sagepub.com/

Farias, S. T., Mungas, D., Reed, B. R., Cahn-Weiner, D., Jagust, W., Baynes, K., & DeCarli, C. (2008). Everyday Cognition Scale. *Psyctests.* doi:10.1037/t04288-000

Finfgeld-Connett, D., & Johnson, E. D. (2013). Literature search strategies for conducting knowledge-building and theory-generating qualitative systematic reviews. *Journal Of Advanced Nursing, 69*(1), 194-204. doi:10.1111/j.1365-2648.2012.06037.x

Federal Way Public Schools. (2016). Retrieved from http://www.fwps.org/domain/224

Fitzgerald, S. (2015). Perceptions of the International Baccalaureate (IB) in Ontario Universities. *Canadian Journal of Education, 38*(3), 1-34. Retrieved from http://www.csse-scee.ca/CJE/

Froman, N. (2015). Human rights education and the International Baccalaureate Diploma Programme. *Current Issues in Comparative Education, 17*(1), 36-58. Retrieved from http://www.tc.columbia.edu/cice

Fornaciari, C. J., & Dean, K. L. (2014). The 21st-century syllabus from pedagogy to andragogy. *Journal of Management Education, 38*(5), 701-723. doi:10.1177/1052562913504763

Fortunati, R., Ossola, P., Camerlengo, A., Bettini, E., Panfilis, C. D., Tonna, M., & ... Marchesi, C. (2015). Anhedonia in schizophrenia: The role of subjective experiences. *Comprehensive Psychiatry, 62*(1), 152-160.

Garza, G. (2007). Varieties of phenomenological research at the University of Dallas: An emerging typology. *Qualitative Research in Psychology, 4*(4), 313. doi:10.1080/14780880701551170

Geake, J. G., & Gross, M. U. (2008). Teachers' negative affect toward academically gifted students an evolutionary psychological study. *Gifted Child Quarterly, 52*(3), 217-231. doi:10.1177/0016986208319704

Gentry, M., Hu, S., & Thomas, A. T. (2008). Ethnically diverse students. In J. Plucker & C. Callahan (Eds.), *Critical issues and practices in gifted education: What the research says* (pp. 195-212). Waco, TX: National Association for Gifted Children.

Germeten, S. (2013). Personal narratives in life history research. *Scandinavian Journal of Educational Research, 57*(6), 612-624. doi:10.1080/00313831.2013.838998

Glaser, B.G. (1978). *Theoretical sensitivity*. Mill Valley, CA: Sociology Press.

Glaser, B. G., & Strauss, A. L. (1967*). The discovery of grounded theory: Strategies for qualitative research.* New York, NY: Aldine de Gruyter.

Gleek, C. (2015). Understanding student engagement during simulations in IB global politics. *IE: Inquiry in Education, 7*(1), 6. Retrieved from http://digitalcommons.nl.edu/ie/

Gökdere, M., Küçük, M., & Çepni, S. (2003). Gifted science education in Turkey: Gifted teachers' selection, perspectives and needs. *Asia-Pacific Forum on Science Learning and Teaching, 4*(2), 5. Retrieved from https://www.ied.edu.hk/apfslt/

Gordon, M., VanderKamp, E., & Halic, O. (2015*). International Baccalaureate programmes in Title I schools in the United States: Accessibility, participation and university enrollment.* Retrieved from http://ibo.org/globalassets/publications/ib-research/title-1-schools-research.pdf

Grañena, G. (2016). Cognitive aptitudes for implicit and explicit learning and information-processing styles: An individual differences study. *Applied Psycholinguistics, 37*(3), 577-600. doi:10.1017/S0142716415000120

Grant, R. M. (2016). *Contemporary strategy analysis: Text and cases edition.* New York, NY: John Wiley & Sons.

Grant, M. (2016). The International Baccalaureate: Guidance counselling, predictions and the Middle Years Program. *International Schools Journal, 35*(2), 76-81. Retrieved from http://www.johncattbookshop.com/books/international-schools-journal.

Hallinger, P., Lee, M., & Walker, A. (2011). Program transition challenges in International Baccalaureate schools. *Journal of Research in International Education, 10*(2), 123-136.

Halic, O., Bergeron, L., Kuvaeva, A., & Smith, A. (2015). The International Baccalaureate's Bilingual Diploma: Global trends, pathways, and predictors of attainment. *International Journal of Educational Research, 69*(1), 59-70. doi:10.1016/j.ijer.2014.10.004

Hasan, M. N. (2016). Positivism: To what extent does it aid our understanding of the contemporary social world? *Quality & Quantity, 50*(1), 317-325. doi:10.1007/s11135-014-0150-4

Hatfield, G. (2014). Activity and passivity in theories of perception: Descartes to Kant. In J. F. Silva, M. Yrjönsuuri, J. F. Silva, M. Yrjönsuuri (Eds.), *Active perception in the history of philosophy: From Plato to modern philosophy* (pp. 275-289). Cham, Switzerland: Springer International Publishing. doi:10.1007/978-3-319-04361-6_15

Hatfield, G. (2014). *The Routledge guidebook to Descartes' meditations.* New York, NY: Routledge.

Hearon, B. V. (2015). *Stress and coping in high school students in accelerated academic curricula: developmental trends and relationships with student success* (Dissertation). Retrieved from Graduate Theses and Dissertations. (5495)

Hertberg-Davis, H., & Callahan, C. M. (2014). Advanced Placement and International Baccalaureate programs. In J. A. Plucker & C. M. Callahan (Eds.), *Critical issues and practices in gifted education: What the research says* (2nd ed., pp. 47-64). Waco, TX: Prufrock Press.

Heidegger, M. (1962). *Being and time.* (J. Macquarrie & E. Robinson, Trans.). Oxford, UK: Blackwell. (Original work published 1927)

Heidegger, M. (2013). *Basic problems of phenomenology:* Winter Semester 1919/1920. (S.M. Campbell, Trans.) New York, NY: Bloomsbury. (Original work published 1919/1920)

Heidegger, M. (2013). *Existence and being.* New York, NY: Read Books.

Heinrich, W. F., Habron, G. B., Johnson, H. L., & Goralnik, L. (2015). Critical thinking assessment across four sustainability-related experiential learning settings. *Journal of Experiential Education, 38*(4), 373-393. doi:10.1177/1053825915592890

Hemelt, S. W. (2014). *The impact of International Baccalaureate's Primary Years Program (PYP) on student performance: Evidence from Michigan and North Carolina (primary years program studies).* Retrieved from http://www.ibo.org/en/about-the-ib/research/research-resources

Heydorn, W., & Jesudason, S. (2013). *Decoding the theory of knowledge.* Cambridge, UK: Cambridge University Press.

Hill, I., & Saxton, S. (2014). The International Baccalaureate (IB) programme: An international gateway to higher education and beyond. *Higher Learning Research Communications, 4*(3), 42. Retrieved from http://www.hlrcjournal.com/index.php/HLRC

Hollingworth, L., & Keuseman, S. H. (2015). How can they be gifted if they don't speak English? Teacher perceptions of the talents of second graders in a dual language program. *Revista Educación y Ciencia (ISSN 2448-525X), 4*(43). Retrieved from http://www.educacionyciencia.org/

Huntington Jr., C. W. (2016). Seeing things as they are. *Tricycle: The Buddhist Review, 25*(3), 38. Retrieved from http://tricycle.org/

Hunt, H. (2013). Implications and consequences of post-modern philosophy for contemporary transpersonal studies: II. Georges Bataille's post-Nietzschean secular mysticism, phenomenology of ecstatic states, and original transpersonal sociology. *International Journal of Transpersonal Studies, 32*(2), 79-97. Retrieved from http://digitalcommons.ciis.edu/ijts-transpersonalstudies/

Husserl, E. (1931). *Ideas.* London, UK: George Allen & Unwin.

Husserl, E. (2002). *Ideas.* (W.R. Boyce Gibson, Trans.). New York, NY: Routledge. (Original work published 1931)

Husserl, E. (2002). Philosophy as rigorous science. *New Yearbook for Phenomenology and Phenomenological Philosophy, 2*, 249-295. Retrieved from https://www.pdcnet.org/nyppp/The-New-Yearbook-for-Phenomenology-and-Phenomenological-Philosophy

International Baccalaureate. (2016). *History of the International Baccalaureate.* Retrieved from http://www.ibo.org/globalassets/digital-tookit/presentations/1503-presentation-historyoftheib-en.pdf

Irizarry, (2015). Selling students short: Racial differences in teachers' evaluations of high, average, and low performing students. *Social Science Research, 52*, 522-538. doi:10.1016/j.ssresearch.2015.04.002

Jamal, S. (2016). From theory to practice: A critical review of the International Baccalaureate Primary Years Program. *International Schools Journal, 35*(2), 22-37. Retrieved from http://www.johncattbookshop.com/books/international-schools-journal

Jedlikowska, D. (2014). Changing roles of teachers in the context of communication: A pedeutological perspective. *Contemporary Educational Researches Journal, 4*(2), 30-34. Retrieved from http://www.world-education-center.org/index.php/cerj

Jones, J. K., & Hébert, T. P. (2012). Engaging diverse gifted learners in U.S. history classrooms. *Gifted Child Today, 35*(4), 252-261. doi:10.1177/1076217512455476

Jordan, T. (2016). Deliberative methods for complex issues: A typology of functions that may need scaffolding. *Group Facilitation: A Research & Applications Journal, 13*(1), 50-71. Retrieved from http://www.albany.edu/cpr/gf/gfj/

Jordan, S., & Lande, M. (2016). Additive innovation in design thinking and making. *International Journal of Engineering Education, 32*(3), 1438-1444. Retrieved from http://www.ijee.ie/

Julmi, C., & Scherm, E. (2015). The domain-specificity of creativity: Insights from new phenomenology. *Creativity Research Journal, 27*(2), 151-159. doi:10.1080/10400419.2015.1030310

Juvova, A., Chudy, S., Neumeister, P., Plischke, J., & Kvintova, J. (2015). Reflection of constructivist theories in current educational practice. *Universal Journal of Educational Research, 3*(5), 345-349. Retrieved from http://www.hrpub.org/journals/jour_info.php?id=95

Kadens, E. (2009). Justice Blackstone's common law orthodoxy. *Northwestern University Law Review,* 1031553.

Kadıoğlu, S., & Erişen, Y. (2016). Analysis of International Baccalaureate Diploma Programme using SWOT in Turkey. *International Online Journal of Educational Sciences, 8*(1), 26-37. doi:10.15345/iojes.2016.01.003

Kahneman, D. (2011). *Thinking, fast and slow*. New York, NY: Macmillan.

Katz, S. (2015). Qualitative-based methodology to teaching qualitative methodology in higher education. *International Journal of Teaching & Learning in Higher Education, 27*(3), 352-363. Retrieved from http://www.isetl.org/ijtlhe/

Park, K., Caine, V., & Wimmer, R. (2014). The Experiences of Advanced Placement and International Baccalaureate Diploma Program Participants: A Systematic Review of Qualitative Research. Journal Of Advanced Academics, 25(2), 129-153. doi:10.1177/1932202X14532258

Kerr, B. (Ed.) (2009). *Encyclopedia of giftedness, creativity, and talent.* Thousand Oaks, CA: Sage. doi:10.4135/9781412971959

Kinghorn, W. (2015). Moral engagement, combat trauma, and the lure of psychiatric dualism: Why psychiatry is more than a technical discipline. *Harvard Review of Psychiatry, 23*(1), 28-37. doi:10.1097/HRP.0000000000000042

Kitsantas, A., & Miller, A. D. (2015*). Characteristics and context of Primary Years Program (PYP) students' self-efficacy and self-regulatory development (primary years program studies).* Retrieved from http://www.ibo.org/globalassets/publications/ib-research/pyp/pyp-self-efficacy-full-report-en.pdf/

Kmansoy, V., & Kartal, S. (2014). Chaos theory and its application to education: Mehmet Akif Ersoy University case. *Educational Sciences: Theory & Practice, 14*(2), 510-518. doi:10.12738/estp.2014.2.1928

Knowles, M. S., Holton III, E. F., & Swanson, R. A. (2014*). The adult learner: The definitive classic in adult education and human resource development.* New York, NY: Routledge.

Creswell (2007) writing in Qualitative inquiry and research design: Choosing among five approaches says five to 25 (p.64).

Kohn, N., & Sydnor, S. (2006). Dialoguing With Norman K. Denzin. *Journal Of Sport & Social Issues,* 30(4), 374-382. doi:10.1177/0193723506293041

Kordeš, U. (2016). Going Beyond Theory. *Constructivist Foundations, 11*(2), 375-385. Retrieved from http://www.constructivistpsych.org/

Kordeš, U. (2016). Where is consciousness? *Constructivist Foundations, 11*(3), 552-554. Retrieved from http://www.constructivistpsych.org/

Kauffman S. (2014). Beyond the stalemate: Conscious mind-body - quantum mechanics - free will - possible panpsychism - possible interpretation of quantum enigma. *Cosmos & History, 10*(1), 149. Ipswich, MA: Supplemental Index.

Kuhn, R. L. (2013). Levels of nothing. *Skeptic, 18*(2), 34-37. Retrieved from http://www.skeptic.com/

Kwan, Y. W., & Wong, A. F. (2015). Effects of the constructivist learning environment on students' critical thinking ability: Cognitive and motivational variables as mediators. *International Journal of Educational Research,* 7068-79. doi:10.1016/j.ijer.2015.02.006

Lahman, M. K., Rodriguez, K. L., Moses, L., Griffin, K. M., Mendoza, B. M., & Yacoub, W. (2015). A rose by any other name is still a rose? Problematizing pseudonyms in research. *Qualitative Inquiry, 21*(5), 445-453. doi:10.1177/1077800415572391

Landis, R. N., & Reschly, A. L. (2013). Reexamining gifted underachievement and dropout through the lens of student engagement. *Journal for the Education of the Gifted, 36*(2), 220-249. doi:10.1177/0162353213480864

Laner, I. I. (2015). Practical aesthetic knowledge: Goodman and Husserl on the possibilities of learning by aesthetic practices. *Estetika: The Central European Journal of Aesthetics, 52*(2), 164-189. Retrieved from http://aesthetics.ff.cuni.cz/

Lanier, L. (2015). *Advanced Maya texturing and lighting.* New York, NY: John Wiley & Sons.

Lather, P. (2007). *Getting lost: Feminist practices toward a double (d) science.* Albany, NY: University at Albany.

Lincoln, Y. S., & Guba, E. G. (1985). *Naturalistic inquiry.* Beverly Hills, CA: Sage.

Lineham, R. (2013). Is the International Baccalaureate Diploma Programme effective at delivering the International Baccalaureate mission statement? *Journal of Research in International Education, 12*(3), 259-282. doi:10.1177/1475240913509765

Lipman, M. (2003). *Thinking in education* (2nd ed.). New York, NY: Cambridge University Press.

Lochmiller, C. R., Lucero, A., & Lester, J. N. (2016). Challenges for a new bilingual program: Implementing the International Baccalaureate Primary Years Programme in four Colombian schools. *Journal of Research in International Education, 15*(2), 155-174. doi:10.1177/1475240916660803

Lüddecke, F. (2016). Philosophically rooted educational authenticity as a normative ideal for education: Is the International Baccalaureate's primary years programme an example of an authentic curriculum? *Educational Philosophy and Theory, 48*(5), 509-524. doi:10.1080/00131857.2015.1041012

Mabrok, M. A., Dong, D., Petersen, I. R., & Chen, C. (2014). Entanglement generation in uncertain quantum systems using sampling-based learning control. *IFAC Proceedings Volumes, 47*(19th IFAC World Congress), 5963-5968. doi:10.3182/20140824-6-ZA-1003.02079

MacRaild, J. (2015). The International Baccalaureate Program: Meeting the needs of high-ability students in Qatar. *TalentEd, 29*(1), 1–17. Retrieved from http://talentedk12.com/

Maggini, G. (2013). Bodily presence, absence, and their ethical challenges. *Techné: Research in Philosophy and Technology, 17*(3), 316-332. doi:10.5840/techne20141297

Makel, M. C., & Wai, J. (2016). Does economic research in education work? For which studies?. *Journal of Advanced Academics, 27*(2), 73-80. doi:10.1177/1932202X15628013

Marchand, G. C., Nardi, N. M., Reynolds, D., & Pamoukov, S. (2014). The impact of the classroom built environment on student perceptions and learning. *Journal of Environmental Psychology, 40*(2), 187-197. doi:10.1016/j.jenvp.2014.06.009

Marshall, G. J. (2008). *A guide to Merleau-Ponty's phenomenology of perception* [electronic resource]. Milwaukee, WI: Marquette University Press.

Mason, M. (2010). Sample Size and Saturation in PhD Studies Using Qualitative Interviews. Forum Qualitative Sozialforschung / Forum: *Qualitative Social Research, 11(3),* 211-219

Matehkolaee, M. J., & Khorasani, S. (2014). The challenging concept of Newtonian mechanics from philosophical view. *Latin-American Journal of Physics Education, 8(4),* 4310-1-43100-4

Matthews, D. J. (2015). Teaching gifted students in regular classrooms: Adapting instruction to meet high level needs. *Caribbean Curriculum, 6*(1), 39-55. Retrieved from http://journals.sta.uwi.edu/cc/

McIntyre, M. M., & Graziano, W. G. (2016). Seeing people, seeing things: Individual differences in selective attention. *Personality & Social Psychology Bulletin, 42*(9), 1258-1271. doi:10.1177/0146167216653937

Menéndez, M. (2015). International Baccalaureate: a supernational curriculum for global citizens. Bordón. Revista de pedagogía, 67(1), 179-194.

Merleau-Ponty, M. (1996). *Phenomenology of perception*. India: Motilal Banarsidass.

Merleau-Ponty, M. (2014). *Fenomenologia della percezione*. Italy: Bompiani.

Meulen, R. R., Bruggen, C., Spilt, J., Verouden, J., Berkhout, M., & Bögels, S. S. (2014). The pullout program day a week school for gifted children: Effects on social-emotional and academic functioning. *Child & Youth Care Forum, 43*(3), 287-314.

Mintz, K., & Tal, T. (2014). Sustainability in higher education courses: Multiple learning outcomes. *Studies in Educational Evaluation, 41*(2), 113-123. doi:10.1016/j.stueduc.2013.11.003

Moore, T. (2013). Critical thinking: Seven definitions in search of a concept. *Studies in Higher Education, 38*(4), 506-522. doi:10.1080/03075079.2011.586995

Moustakas, C. E. (1994). *Phenomenological research methods*. Thousand Oaks, CA: Sage.

Moustakas, C. E. (1995). *Being-in, being-for, being-with*. New York, NY: Jason Aronson.

Munro, G. D., & Munro, C. A. (2014). 'Soft' versus 'hard' psychological science: Biased evaluations of scientific evidence that threatens or supports a strongly held political identity. *Basic and Applied Social Psychology, 36*(6), 533-543. doi:10.1080/01973533.2014.960080

Nader, J., & Woodrow Wilson International Center for Scholars. (2008). Stakeholders in student success: Public-private partnerships strengthening K-12 education. Washington, DC: Woodrow Wilson International Center for Scholars.

Narlikar, J. V. (2015). The early days of general relativity. *Current Science (00113891), 109*(12), 2214-2219. doi:10.18520/v109/i12/2214-2219

National Association for Gifted Children. (2010). *Redefining giftedness for a new century: Shifting the paradigm* (Position paper). Washington, DC: Author.

National Association of Gifted Children. (2016). *Definitions of giftedness*. Retrieved from http://www.nagc.org/resources-publications/resources/definitions-giftedness

National Council for Excellence in Critical Thinking. (2016). Retrieved from
http://www.criticalthinking.org/pages/the-national-council-for-excellence-in-critical-
thinking/406

Nixon, E., & Gabriel, Y. (2016). 'So much choice and no choice at all.' *Marketing Theory,*
16(1), 39. doi:10.1177/1470593115593624

Nixon, L. F. (2016). Creativity and positive disintegration. *Advanced Development, 15*(1), 12-31.
Retrieved from http://www.gifteddevelopment.com/product-category/advanced-
development-journal

No Child Left Behind Act, P.L. 107-110. Title IX, Part A, Definitions (22) (2002); 20 U.S.C.
Sec. 7802 (22).

O'Brien, D. T. (2012). Thinking, fast and slow by Daniel Kahneman. *Journal of Social,*
Evolutionary, and Cultural Psychology, 6(2), 253-256. doi:10.1037/h0099210

O'Brien, K. (2012). Global environmental change II From adaptation to deliberate
transformation. *Progress in Human Geography, 36*(5), 667-676.
doi:10.1177/0309132511425767

O'Reilly, M., & Parker, N. (2012). Unsatisfactory saturation: A critical
exploration of the notion of saturated sample sizes in qualitative research.
Qualitative Research, 13(2), 190-197. doi:10.1177/1468794112446106

Ozcan, D., & Kotek, A. (2015). What do the teachers think about gifted students?. *Procedia-*
Social and Behavioral Sciences, 190, 569-573. doi:10.1016/j.sbspro.2015.05.044

Ozcan, D., Besgul, M., Kaptanoglu, H., & Argun, S. (2015). Examination of Primary School
Teachers' Opinions about Gifted Students. *Procedia - Social And Behavioral Sciences,*
190, 416-424. doi:10.1016/j.sbspro.2015.05.019

Ozcan, D., & Zabadi, T. I. (2015). Comparison of public and private school teachers and school
principals opinions in Abuja, Nigeria. *Cypriot Journal of Educational Sciences, 10*(1),
53-64. Retrieved from http://www.world-education-center.org/index.php/cjes

Packer, M. (2011). *The science of qualitative research.* Cambridge, UK: Cambridge University
Press.

Pálffy, A. (2012). Quantum enigma: Physics encounters consciousness, 2nd ed., by Bruce
Rosenblum and Fred Kuttner. *Contemporary Physics, 53*(3), 282.
doi:10.1080/00107514.2012.661786

Park, K., Caine, V., & Wimmer, R. (2014). The experiences of advanced placement and
international baccalaureate diploma program participants: A systematic review of
qualitative research. *Journal of Advanced Academics, 25*(2), 129-153.
doi:10.1177/1932202X14532258

Perna, L. W., Orosz, K., Jumakulov, Z., Kishkentayeva, M., & Ashirbekov, A. (2015). Understanding the programmatic and contextual forces that influence participation in a government-sponsored international student-mobility program. *Higher Education, 69*(2), 173-188. doi:10.1007/s10734-014-9767-4

Peterson, A. D. C. (2003). *Schools across frontiers: The story of the International Baccalaureate and the United World Colleges*. Chicago, IL: Open Court.

Pinker, S. (2011). *The better angels of our nature: Why violence has declined* (Vol. 75). New York, NY: Viking.

Pitre, N. (2015). *Four Canadian expatriate women's personal history self-study stories on their International-Mindedness (IM) development and approaches to teaching IM* (Doctoral dissertation). Canada, University of Calgary.

Plucker, J. A., & Callahan, C. M. (2014). Research on giftedness and gifted education status of the field and considerations for the future. *Exceptional Children, 80*(4), 390-406. doi:10.1177/0014402914527244

Plunkett, M., & Kronborg, L. (2011). Learning to be a teacher of the gifted: The importance of examining opinions and challenging misconceptions. *Gifted and Talented International, 26*(1-2), 31-46. doi:10.1080/15332276.2011.11673587

Polowczyk, J. (2013). Thinking fast and slow. *The Poznan University of Economics Review, 13*(3), 130. Retrieved from http://www.puereview.ue.poznan.pl/index.php/en/

Ponte, M. M. (2012) *Phenomenology of perception* (D.A. Landes, Trans.). New York, NY: Routledge. (Original work published 1945)

Poonoosamy, M. (2015). Aspirations and tensions in developing international mindedness: Case study of two students in an IB school in an Indian Ocean Island Nation. *Asia Pacific Journal of Education, 36*(4), 1-16. doi:10.1080/02188791.2015.1064354

Preckel, F., Götz, T., & Frenzel, A. (2010). Ability grouping of gifted students: Effects on academic self-concept and boredom. *British Journal of Educational Psychology, 80*(3), 451-472. doi:10.1348/000709909X480716

Quaynor, L. (2015). Liberia: Citizenship education in the Post-Conflict Era. In E. Takyi-Amoako (Ed.), *Education in West Africa* (pp. 283-290). New York, NY: Routledge.

Rajan, S., Khanna, A., Argalious, M., Kimatian, S. J., Mascha, E. J., Makarova, N., & ... Avitsian, R. (2016). Comparison of 2 resident learning tools—interactive screen-based simulated case scenarios versus problem-based learning discussions: a prospective quasi-crossover cohort study. *Journal of Clinical Anesthesia, 28*4-11. doi:10.1016/j.jclinane.2015.08.003

Roberts, J. L., Pereira, N., & Knotts, J. D. (2015). State law and policy related to twice-exceptional learners. *Gifted Child Today, 38*(4), 215-219. doi:10.1177/1076217515597276

Rowe, E. W., Dandridge, J., Pawlush, A., Thompson, D. F., & Ferrier, D. E. (2014). Exploratory and confirmatory factor analyses of the WISC-IV with gifted students. *School Psychology Quarterly, 29*(4), 536-552. doi:10.1037/spq0000009

Riener, C. (2015). Seeing is the hardest thing to see: Using illusions to teach visual perception. *New Directions for Teaching & Learning, 2015*(141), 43-51. doi:10.1002/tl.20121

Reis, S. M., Baum, S. M., & Burke, E. (2014). An operational definition of twice-exceptional learners implications and applications. *Gifted Child Quarterly, 58*(3), 217-230. doi:10.1177/0016986214534976

Reiss, K. (2014). *Translation criticism-potentials and limitations: Categories and criteria for translation quality assessment.* New York, NY: Routledge.

Reiss, T. J. (2014). The matter of mind: Reason and experience in the age of Descartes. *Modern Language Quarterly, 75*(4), 581-586. doi:10.1215/00267929-2798018

Resnik, J. (2012). The denationalization of education and the expansion of the International Baccalaureate. *Comparative Education Review, 56*(2), 248-269. Retrieved from http://www.journals.uchicago.edu/toc/cer/current

Ricci, G. R. (2015). Edmund Husserl's reception in Marvin Farber's philosophy and phenomenological research. *Journal of Scholarly Publishing, 46*(3), 265-281. doi:10.3138/jsp.46.3.04

Richards, C. (2015). Outcomes-based authentic learning, portfolio assessment, and a systems approach to 'Complex Problem-Solving:' Related pillars for enhancing the innovative role of PBL in future higher education. *Journal of Problem Based Learning in Higher Education, 3*(1), 1-12. doi:10.5278/ojs.jpblhe.v3i1.1204

Richardson, K., & Norgate, S. H. (2015). Does IQ really predict job performance? *Applied Developmental Science, 19*(3), 153-169. doi:10.1080/10888691.2014.983635

Rosenblum, B., & Kuttner, F. (2011). *Quantum enigma: Physics encounters consciousness.* New York, NY: Oxford University Press..

Russell, B. (2013). *Human knowledge: Its scope and value.* New York, NY: Routledge.

Russell, H. A. (2013). Quantum anthropology: Reimaging the human person as body/spirit. *Theological Studies, 74*(4), 934-959. Retrieved from http://theologicalstudies.net/

Saavedra, A. R. (2014). The academic impact of enrollment in International Baccalaureate diploma programs: A case study of Chicago public schools. *Teachers College Record, 116*(4), n4. Retrieved from http://www.tcrecord.org

Saldana, J. (2013). *The coding manual for qualitative* researchers (2nd ed.). Thousand Oaks, CA: Sage.

Sanders, H. F. (2015). *Phenomenological study of Mexican parents conceptualization of education related to student success* (Doctoral dissertation). University of Phoenix, Tempe, AZ. (3736715)

Sanders, R. (2015). A historical perspective on modified Newtonian dynamics. *Canadian Journal of Physics, 93*(2), 126-138. Retrieved from http://www.nrcresearchpress.com/journal/cjp

Schmidt, H. (2014, Winter). Structuralism in Physics. *The Stanford Encyclopedia of Philosophy*. Retrieved from http://plato.stanford.edu/archives/win2014/entries/physics-structura

Schmitt, C., & Goebel, V. (2015). Experiences of high-ability high school students. *Journal for the Education of the Gifted, 38*(4), 428-446. doi:10.1177/0162353215607325

Schutz, A. (1962). *The problem of social reality: collected papers I*. The Hague: Martinus Nijhoff.

Shi, Z. (2011). Dilemmas in using phenomenology to investigate elementary school children learning English as a second language. *In education, 17*(1), 3-13.

Siegle, D., Gubbins, E. J., O'Rourke, P., Langley, S. D., Mun, R. U., Luria, S. R., & ... Plucker, J. A. (2016). Barriers to underserved students' participation in gifted programs and possible solutions. *Journal for the Education of the Gifted, 39*(2), 103-131. doi:10.1177/0162353216640930

Silverman, D. (2013). *Doing qualitative research* (4th ed.). Thousand Oaks, CA: Sage.

Smith, D. L. (1996). The evolution of Duquesne University's project for a human science psychology. *The Humanistic Psychologist, 24*(1), 79-94. doi:10.1080/08873267.1996.9986843

Smith, N. V., & Morgan, M. (2010). Politics and pedagogy: Discursive constructions in the IB theory of knowledge. *Curriculum Journal, 21*(3), 299-312. doi:10.1080/09585176.2010.504576

Snyder, T. D., Dillow, S. A., & National Center for Education Statistics. (2015). *Digest of Education Statistics 2013*. Washington, DC: National Center for Education Statistics.

Stake, R. E. (1995). *The art of case study research*. Thousand Oaks, CA: Sage.

Stake, R., & Munson, A. (2008). Qualitative assessment of arts education. *Arts Education Policy Review, 109*(6), 13-21. doi:10.3200/AEPR.109.6.13-22.

Steenbergen-Hu, S., & Olszewski-Kubilius, P. (2016). Gifted Identification and the Role of Gifted Education. *Journal of Advanced Academics, 27*(2), 99-108. doi:10.1177/1932202X16643836

Steiner, R. (2011). *The philosophy of freedom* (R.F. Hoernle, Trans.). Vienna, Austria: Steiner. (Original work published 1916)

Steiner, R. (2001). *The renewal of education* (Anthroposophic Press, Trans.). Great Barrington, MA: Anthroposophic Press. (Original work published 1920)

Strauss, A. L. (1987). *Qualitative analysis for social sciences.* Cambridge, UK: Cambridge University Press.

Strauss, A., & Corbin, J. (1998). *Basics of qualitative research: Techniques and procedures for developing grounded theory* (2nd ed.). Thousand Oaks, CA: Sage.

Subotnik, R. F., Olszewski-Kubilius, P., & Worrell, F. C. (2011). Rethinking giftedness and gifted education: A proposed direction forward based on psychological science. *Psychological Science in the Public Interest, 12*(1), 3-54. doi:10.1177/1529100611418056

Swan, B., Coulombe-Quach, X., Huang, A., Godek, J., Becker, D., & Zhou, Y. (2015). Meeting the Needs of Gifted and Talented Students. *Journal of Advanced Academics,* 26(4), 294-319. doi:10.1177/1932202X15603366

Sweet, A. A., Sweet, C. F., & Jaensch, F. (2016). Response to Stuart Kauffman: The paradox of divine action and scientific truth. *Theology & Science, 14*(1), 59-64. doi:10.1080/14746700.2015.1122327

Tarhan, O. (2015). The state of in-service training of teachers and teacher training in National Education Councils. *Procedia - Social and Behavioral Sciences, 197,* 378-381. doi:10.1016/j.sbspro.2015.07.152

Tahhan, D. A. (2013). Touching at depth: The potential of feeling and connection. *Emotion, Space, and Society, 7*(1), 45-53. doi:10.1016/j.emospa.2012.03.004

Tarc, P., & Beatty, L. (2012). The emergence of the International Baccalaureate Diploma in Ontario: Diffusion, pilot study and prospective research. *Canadian Journal of Education, 35*(4), 341-375. Retrieved from http://www.cje-rce.ca/

Thomas, T. (2011). Developing first year students' critical thinking skills. *Asian Social Science, 7*(4), 26-35. Retrieved from http://www.ccsenet.org/journal/index.php/ass

Tong, E. W. (2016). Spirituality and the temporal dynamics of transcendental positive emotions. *Psychology of Religion and Spirituality, 8*(1). doi:10.1037/rel0000061

The National Council for Excellence in Critical Thinking. (2016*). The critical thinking community.* Retrieved from http://www.criticalthinking.org/pages/the-national-council-for-excellence-in-critical-thinking/406

Trott, A. M. (2013). Ruling in turn: Political rule against mastery in Aristotle's politics. *Epoché: A Journal for the History of Philosophy, 17*(2), 301-311. doi:10.5840/epoche201317210

U.S. Department of Education Office for Civil Rights. (2014). *Civil rights data collection.* Retrieved from http://ocrdata.ed.gov/Downloads/CRDC-School-Discipline-Snapshot.pdf

Vall Castelló, B. (2016). Bridging constructivism and social constructionism: The journey from narrative to dialogical approaches and towards synchrony. *Journal of Psychotherapy Integration, 26*(2), 129-143. doi:10.1037/int0000025

Vanderbrook, C. M. (2006). Intellectually gifted females and their perspectives of lived experience in the AP and IB programs. *Prufrock Journal, 17*(3), 133-148. doi:10.4219/jsge-2006-396

Van Oord, L. (2013). Moral education and the International Baccalaureate learner profile. *Educational Studies (03055698), 39*(2), 208. doi:10.1080/03055698.2012.717260

Vogl, K., & Preckel, F. (2014). Full-time ability grouping of gifted students impacts on social self-concept and school-related attitudes. *Gifted Child Quarterly, 58*(1), 51-68. doi:10.1177/0016986213513795

Weingarten, R. (2014). International Education Comparisons: How American Education Reform Is the New Status Quo. *New England Journal of Public Policy, 26*(1), 1-10.

Wellmer, A. (2014). On critical theory. *Social Research, 81*(3), 705-733. doi:10.1353/sor.2014.0045

Wenger, E., McDermott, R., & Snyder, W. M. (2002). *Cultivating communities of practice: A guide to managing knowledge.* Boston, MA: Harvard Business School.

Wickson, F., Strand, R., & Kjølberg, K. L. (2015). The walkshop approach to science and technology ethics. *Science and Engineering Ethics, 21*(1), 241-264. doi:10.1007/s11948-014-9526-z

Willig, C. (2008). Discourse analysis. In J.A. Smith (Ed.), *Qualitative psychology: A practical guide to research methods* (2nd ed.; pp. 160-85). London, UK: Sage.

Wintergerst, A. C., DeCapua, A., & Verna, M. A. (2003). Conceptualizing learning style modalities for ESL/EFL students. *System, 31*(1), 85-106. doi:10.1016/S0346-251X(02)00075-1

Winebrenner, S. (1999). Shortchanging the gifted. *School Administrator, 56*(9), 12-16. Retrieved from http://www.aasa.org/SchoolAdministrator.aspx

Woelders, S., & Abma, T. (2015). A different light on normalization: Critical theory and responsive evaluation studying social justice in participation practices. *New Directions for Evaluation, 2015*(146), 9-18. doi:10.1002/ev.20116

Wolanin, N., & Wade, J. (2015). *Evaluation of the Howard Hughes Science Grant Project, year one.* Rockville, MD: Montgomery County Public Schools.

Webb, J. T. (1994). *Nurturing social emotional development of gifted children.* Reston, VA: ERIC Clearinghouse.

Wright, E., & Lee, M. (2014). Elite International Baccalaureate Diploma Programme schools and inter-cultural understanding in China. *British Journal of Educational Studies, 62*(2), 149-169. doi:10.1080/00071005.2014.924615

Wright, K. (2015). *International baccalaureate programmes: Longer-term outcomes.* Retrieved from http://test-ibexternalweb.customers.nansen.se/globalassets/publications/ib-research/continuum/longer-term-outcomes-final-en.pdf

Wu, G. (2015). Questioning of quantum information. In ISIS Summit Vienna 2015—*The Information Society at the Crossroads.* Basel, Switzerland: Multidisciplinary Digital Publishing Institute.

Wu, R. (2015). Heidegger's concept of being-in-the-πόλις. *The Humanistic Psychologist, 43*(3), 267-277. doi:10.1080/08873267.2015.1031900

Zeidner, M., Shani-Zinovich, I., Matthews, G., & Roberts, R. D. (2005). Assessing emotional intelligence in gifted and non-gifted high school students: Outcomes depend on the measure. *Intelligence, 33369-391.* doi:10.1016/j.intell.2005.03.001

Zarestky, J. (2016). Escaping preconceived notions. *Adult Learning, 27*(2), 84-86. doi:10.1177/1045159515594182

Appendix A: Student Interview Questions

Describe your understanding of Phenomenology, and Transcendental Phenomenology in an education learning context using the following descriptions:

1. **Phenomenology:** Phenomenology is a science movement dealing with the abstraction of existence. In this discipline, object awareness is an intellection of reality (Julmi & Scherm, 2015). (Or, if a husband makes a statement in a quiet wood, and his wife is not there to hear him, is he still wrong? :)

2. **Transcendental Phenomenology:** Transcendental Phenomenology is the reasoning claim that a sub-conclusion or conclusion is a presupposition and necessary condition of a premise. That priori *(being without examination or analysis)* concepts, through evolutionary process, apply to intentions playing a part in our experience (Moustakas, 1995). (Or, somehow, I have been here before.)

3. **And, Finally:**

In the TOK *Ship of Theseus* thought experiment, could an IB DP student be on the ship and in class at the same time?

OR:

Can a person be in two places at once?

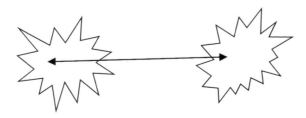

4. Describe your overall school experience including other schools you attended.5

Identify your personal graduation experience.

6. Discuss why you chose your school or was it chosen for you?

7. In your opinion, and in the opinion of your friends, how does your school compare to other schools within your community?

8. Describe yourself as a student scholar, as a student, as a learner.

9. How do you describe your high school experience to your friends?

10. What part of your school experience did you enjoy most?

11. When in school, did you understand the education philosophy of your school?

12. How does course material maintain your interest?

13. When you were bored in school did you blame the school?

14. What made your school special?

15. What does your school mean to you?

16. How has your school affected your worldview?

17. Describe the relationship between you and members of the faculty.

18. Do you feel there was an overemphasis on the arts in your school?

19. As a student did you have input in your own education at your school?

20. Has your school been important to your socialization in society?

121. Going forward will your school have been increasing or diminishing importance?

22. Given the option, would you have attended another school?

74409874R00085

Made in the USA
Columbia, SC
30 July 2017